A Note from the Editor

You are about to take a journey backward in time. Your means of transportation will be the written word and some glorious photographs. Your journey will take you, decade by decade, through the 20th century . . . our century.

Many of the events described in each issue of *Our Century* magazine are famous. Some have perhaps been forgotten. Many of the people were extraordinary, some merely ordinary, a few certainly evil. But all these events and people have one thing in common: they have made this century a fascinating and momentous one.

All of us who worked on *Our Century* hope you find your journey into the past interesting and educational. And most of all we hope you enjoy these "snapshots in time" as much as we enjoyed recapturing them for you.

Tony Napoli

Tony Napoli, Editor-in-Chief, *Our Century*

Statistics

	1970	1980
Population of the United States	203.3 million	226.5 million
Number of states in the United States	50	50
Population by race:		
White	178.0 million	194.8 million
Black	22.5 million	26.6 million
Other	2.8 million	5.1 million
Population by sex:		
Male	98.9 million	110 million
Female	104.4 million	116.5 million
Population per square mile	57.5	64.0
Life expectancy:		
Male	67.1	70.7
Female	74.8	78.1
Number of homicides	16,848	24,278
Number of visitors to national parks and monuments	45.9 million	60.2 million
Number of post offices	32,002	30,326
Number of movie theaters	14,000	18,000
Number of radio stations:		
AM	4,323	4,589
FM	2,767	3,282
Number of daily newspapers	1,763	1,775
Number of passenger cars sold	8,405,000	8,979,000
Number of domestic telephones	56 million	59 million
Number of households with television sets	58.5 million	76.3 million
Number of households with VCRs	0	1.1 million
Number of junior colleges	892	1,274
Number of students graduating from high school	2,896,000	3,133,000
Unemployment rate	4.9%	6.9%
Average hourly wage	$3.23	$6.66
Prices:		
dozen eggs	61¢	72¢
quart of milk	33¢	41¢
loaf of bread	24¢	36¢
pound of butter	87¢	$1.01
pound of coffee	91¢	$1.09
dozen oranges	86¢	96¢

OUR CENTURY

By Prescott Hill
Designer: Detta Penna

Photographs: All cover photos and pp. 4-48, 50, 51 (bottom), 52-57, 59 (top), 60-63: UPI/Bettmann Newsphotos; pp. 51 (top), 59 (bottom): UPI/Bettmann Archive; p.49: Courtesy of Apple Computer, Inc., p. 58: Springer/Bettmann Film Archive; p. 64: AP/Wide World Photos. Advertisements on endpapers: The D'Arcy Collection, University of Illinois at Urbana-Champaign.

1970-1980

For a free color catalog describing Gareth Stevens' list of high-quality books, call 1-800-542-2595 (USA) or
1-800-461-9120 (Canada). Gareth Stevens' Fax: (414) 225-0377.

Library of Congress Cataloging-in-Publication Data

Our century.
      p. cm.
      Originally published: Belmont, Calif.: Fearon Education, 1989.
      Includes bibliographical references and index.
      Contents: [1] 1900-1910/written by Janice Green—[2] 1910-1920/written by Karen Liberatore—[3] 1920-1930/written by Prescott Hill—[4] 1930-1940/
written by Marna Owen—[5] 1940-1950/written by Prescott Hill—[6] 1950-1960/written by S.D. Jones—[7] 1960-1970/written by Joyce Lane—
[8] 1970-1980/written by Prescott Hill—[9] 1980-1990/written by Joanne Suter.
      ISBN 0-8368-1039-2 [8]
      1. Civilization, Modern—20th century—Juvenile literature. [1. History, Modern—20th century. 2. Civilization, Modern—20th century.]
CB425.097 1993
909.82—dc20   93-11445

This North American edition published by
Gareth Stevens Publishing
1555 North RiverCenter Drive, Suite 201
Milwaukee, Wisconsin 53212, USA

This edition first published in 1993 by Gareth Stevens, Inc. Originally published in 1989 by Fearon Education, 500 Harbor Boulevard,
Belmont, California, 94002, with © 1989 by Fearon Education. End matter © 1993 by Gareth Stevens, Inc.

Printed in the United States of America

 3 4 5 6 7 8 9 99 98 97 96

Gareth Stevens Publishing
MILWAUKEE

Police escorted buses of black students to school in Boston in 1974.

Education

Schools Face Many Problems

For years the little red schoolhouse had been a symbol of American education. But as the 1970s began, a better symbol might have been a bottle of red ink. American schools—public and private—were having money problems.

Inflation was one reason for the trouble. Everyone could see that the cost of running a household was rising. So it was no surprise that the cost of running a school was rising too. Utility bills were higher. Teacher's salaries were higher. The cost of insurance was higher. These costs affected the budgets of existing schools. The cost of building new schools was staggering.

In 1965, New York University planned to construct four new buildings. At the time, the cost was projected to be $37 million. But by 1971, the price tag had increased to $52 million.

School districts tightened their belts. Across the nation they cut back on "extras." Often that meant dropping music, arts, and sports programs. Some schools even reduced the number of days they were in session.

School administrators and teachers felt that the federal government should contribute more. The National Education Association (NEA), thought Washington should pay a full one-third of school budgets. In 1971 the federal government was kicking in less than one-tenth.

For teachers, getting a raise was a problem. And it was getting harder for teachers to find jobs. Attendance was down in schools. Children born in the postwar baby boom were almost grown. Lower attendance meant fewer jobs for teachers.

The NEA recommended that schools have smaller classes. This would lower the teacher-student ratio. Students would get more attention and there'd be more jobs for teachers. But that solution would cost more money. And where it would come from, no one knew.

Racial Problems Increase

Money wasn't the only problem in American education. School desegregation had been the law of the land since 1954. But two decades later, many Americans were still angrily resisting integration. The target of their anger was the use of busing to integrate schools.

Violence flared as the 1975–76 school year started in Louisville, Kentucky. As a protest against busing, thousands of people raided school campuses. They threw rocks and burned school buses. National Guardsmen and state police finally quieted the mobs. But the protests continued. Four weeks after the riots, some 3,000 people marched through the streets. Their signs demanded: "Stop Busing!"

In years gone by, such incidents

Integration of elementary schools through forced busing caused protests and unrest in many American cities during the decade.

had usually been associated with the South. But in the mid-'70s, they occurred more often in the North. South Boston, an Irish-Catholic stronghold, resisted busing violently. Police finally controlled the angry mobs. But there, as in Louisville, the protests lingered on.

Two weeks after the opening day of school, Boston's school problems grew worse. Teachers went out on strike for better hours, better pay, and better working conditions. And the trouble wasn't only in Boston. Teachers struck across the country, in big cities and small towns. New York schools were shut down for a week. In Chicago, the teachers' strike lasted 11 days.

As problems in the schools grew worse, so did the nation's drug problem. Many of the "flower children" of the 1960s used illegal drugs like marijuana and LSD as part of their wild and free life style. Now young people of the 1970s were using "speed"—amphetamines—and barbiturates, or "downers." Amphetamines

and barbiturates had great potential for abuse. Dangerous as they were, both were legal. With a prescription, they could be purchased in any drugstore.

Police and school officials were particularly worried about a new illegal drug. It was called PCP. People under its influence often behaved violently.

During the sixties, alcohol seemed to have lost popularity on campuses. But that changed in the 1970s. Studies by the National Institute of Alcohol Abuse and Alcoholism indicated that drinking alcohol was back. Not only was student drinking increasing, it was starting at an earlier age. A 1974 study indicated that "more than half the nation's seventh graders had tried drinking."

The troubles America's schools faced during the 1970s continued throughout the decade. And educators—as well as parents and government officials—continued to search for solutions. ■

Frustrations of Modern Living . . . '70s Style

BLACKOUTS

In July 1977, New York suffered its second major blackout in the past 15 years. Unlike the first time, however, the city did not remain peaceful. There was widespread looting and vandalism. Some 2,000 stores were stripped by looters. About 4,000 people were arrested and nearly 500 police officers were injured. Nine million people went without electrical power for 25 hours. ∎

WALKOUTS

Anyone who lived in a city in 1975 probably went without some kind of city service for a while. During that year city workers all across the country walked off their jobs for one reason or another. In San Francisco it was the police; in Chicago and Charleston, West Virginia, it was the teachers; in New York it was the doctors and the sanitation workers. And these were just a few of the dozens of city strikes to inconvenience citizens that year. For some city dwellers, such as this New York woman, even mailing a letter could turn out to be a real adventure. ∎

AIR POLLUTION

The problem of air pollution continued to plague many large cities during the decade. The combination of wastes from factories and cars often created heavy smog that endangered people's health. At the beginning of the decade, the federal government took steps to help clean up the air in America's cities. In 1970 Congress passed the Clean Air Amendments. These laws required that hydrocarbon and carbon monoxide emissions be reduced in all automobiles manufactured after 1974.

The government also began to act directly against industrial polluters that failed to comply with state pollution rules. Still, city dwellers were often faced with severe health hazards. Pictured here are citizens of Los Angeles during a heavy smog siege in 1979. Even with tougher government rules, air pollution promised to be a problem well into the 1980s. ■

GAS LINES

Throughout the latter part of the decade, gasoline prices rose to unheard of levels. By 1979, not only were prices high, but the energy "crisis" had caused a gasoline shortage. Or so the American people were told. California began an alternate-day plan of gasoline rationing. Was your license plate odd or even? That's what determined which days you could buy gas. This remedy immediately caused huge backups at gas stations such as this one. Many doubted whether the gas "crunch" was real. But before long, many other states followed California's plan. And soon, Americans across the country were waiting in yet another long line—and wondering what wonderful surprises the 1980s might bring. ■

In 1970 maxidresses and fringed trousers signaled the end of the high-hemmed miniskirt of the '60s.

Fashion

From Dresses to Sideburns, Long Is In

Fashion in the 1970s got off to a bad start. At least that's what most men thought. The miniskirt of the sixties had delighted women watchers. But now, according to fashion designers, the supershort skirt was out of style. "Women are definitely ready for a fashion change," said designer Leo Narducci.

Designer Adele Simpson said, "It's goodbye thigh."

Designer James Galanos said, "Long is where the direction is."

The 1970 spring collection reflected the longer look. The hems of most skirts and dresses fell somewhere around the knee. Fashion reporters called the longer styles "longuettes," but everybody else called them midis. But even worse times were ahead for men who bemoaned the passing of the mini. It came in the form of the maxi. The maxi practically tickled the insteps of the wearer. And it didn't do much for the viewer. By the mid-1970s, though, most dresses were neither mini nor maxi. They weren't even midi.

Consider the dress Rosalyn Carter wore at her husband's inauguration in 1977. Its hem fell just below the knee. But the Associated

Press didn't bother to give it a name. To them, as to most people, it was just a blue dress.

For men, the 1970s brought the polyester leisure suit. It was supposed to be a cross between casual wear and business wear. The leisure suit was defined by its fabric as much as by its style. Usually it was made of polyester and featured stretchy fastenings. Its colors were generally garish. Like the Nehru jackets of the sixties, the leisure suit had one good feature: it didn't stay around long.

If anything characterized men's styles in the sixties, it was hair length. Wearing long hair was the surest way to prove you were a rebel. Long sideburns helped, too.

In the seventies though, lots of hair didn't mean you were a hippie. Establishment men started showing off their hair, too. In baseball, the most conservative of sports, long sideburns became popular. Even stars like Pete Rose had them. By the end of the decade, sideburns belonged to the establishment. As an example, consider the presidents.

In 1970, Richard Nixon's sideburns were level with the top of his ear. In 1975, Gerald Ford's sideburns ended at the middle of his ear. In 1979, Jimmy Carter's sideburns reached to the bottom of his ear.

By presidential decree, it seemed, sideburns were in. But that, of course, meant nothing. Though the establishment follows fashion, fashion doesn't follow it.

The last fashion of the 1970s—and certainly the strongest —was Punk.

The Punk look started in London in the mid-1970s. It was first popular with unemployed teenagers and students. Its basic premise seemed to be: the worse you looked the better.

In Punk, a half-shaved head looked twice as good as one with a neat haircut. Dyed hair was in, so long as it stuck out at odd angles. Green and purple were favorite colors.

Torn and dirty clothing was particularly stylish. The leading accessory was the safety pin. It held ripped clothing together and was even worn through the cheek or ear.

The Punk style was meant to offend. It began as a protest against sterile, establishment fashions. But fashion is fickle. By the end of the 1970s, the establishment itself was taking up a version of the Punk look. ■

One designer said, "It's goodbye thigh."

This rather outrageous evening suit—close-fitting tunic jacket with hand-painted gold pattern—made its fashion debut in 1972.

Vietnam '70

The More Things Change, the More They Stay the Same

For the first third of 1970, the Vietnam War went on pretty much as usual. There were no major battles or campaigns. Neither side seemed to gain an advantage. Still, the character of the war was undergoing a change. Fewer Americans were engaged in the fighting.

Then on April 30, 1970, President Nixon sent 30,000 troops into Cambodia. For two months the U.S. government supported Cambodian leader Lon Nol. He was fighting the North Vietnamese who occupied eastern Cambodia.

At the end of June, Nixon termed the Cambodian campaign a success. About 340 Americans and some 800 South Vietnamese had died in the fighting. But the U.S. government claimed to have killed more than 11,000 Communist soldiers. And, they also captured a vast collection of supplies.

In Paris, peace talks seemed to be getting nowhere. But all the while, American troops continued to pull out of Vietnam. It appeared that the Americans were willing to withdraw quietly. One condition, though, had to be met. All POWs had to be released.

The importance of the prisoners of war was emphasized in November 1970. In a daring raid, Americans attacked a POW camp in North Vietnam. It was within 25 miles of Hanoi. Unfortunately, they didn't find any American prisoners there.

A trooper of the U.S. First Cavalry charges between rubber trees during an assault on a Vietcong bunker just east of Dua Thieng.

A South Vietnamese soldier flings a grenade at the enemy. The fighting took place about 22 miles from Saigon, in October 1972.

Just before the raid, Nixon had ordered heavy bombing in North Vietnam. The Communists said it violated an agreement to halt the bombing. But Nixon disagreed with them. In December he gave the Communists a warning: If they heated up the war, he'd increase the bombing in the North even more.

The only good news had to do with American withdrawals. As the year ended, the number of Americans in Vietnam had almost been cut in half.

American troop involvement had peaked in April 1969. Then, there were about 543,000 American troops in Vietnam. At the end of 1970, though, there were only 340,000. And there was more good news. Nixon promised to pull 60,000 more troops out by May 1971.

U.S. Morale Drops

Perhaps the worst news for the United States had to do with troop morale. The attitude of American troops had undergone a change. They knew they were going to be pulled out soon. Many resented having to continue fighting. It seemed that America was no longer committed to victory. So why should they still have

---

The only good news had to do with American troop withdrawals.

---

to fight and die? Morale sank. Discipline and drug problems increased.

There were other reasons for the fall in morale. Many of the South Vietnamese wanted America out. They had come to believe that the American presence only made peace less likely. They held anti-American demonstrations in the streets of

Saigon. That created more resentment among American troops. Already 44,000 Americans had died fighting for South Vietnam. Why go on fighting for such ungrateful people?

As the war dragged on, government leaders kept two main goals in mind. The first was to replace American troops with South Vietnamese forces. The second was to restore stability to the countryside.

The troop replacement—called Vietnamization—was working well. But the struggle for control of the country was less successful. Most people doubted the claim that 95% of the country was in government hands.

Villagers didn't report Communist infiltrators to the government. Many Americans believed the Communists were just waiting for the U.S. troops to leave. Then they'd easily beat the South Vietnamese army.   ⇨

In April 1972, wounded South Vietnamese troops were fended off as they tried to board a helicopter at An Loc. The helicopter had just brought in fresh troops.

South Vietnam's president Nguyen Van Thieu didn't think that was so. He felt the war was cooling down. He said it would be "a relatively minor frontier action in three years."

In the meantime, though, Thieu's government needed more money. That created a problem. Americans had grown disgusted with the corruption in South Vietnam's government. Always, they seemed to want more money. Some members of Congress thought America might just as well be throwing the money away. But American officials in Vietnam supported Thieu. They believed that without the money, the war would be lost. If that happened, those 44,000 American lives really would have been wasted.

That didn't satisfy critics. They said it wasn't enough just to train and equip Thieu's troops. Even if they were strong militarily, could they get the people's backing?

Popular acceptance had been a problem from the beginning. The South Vietnamese couldn't seem to reform their government. If they didn't treat their people fairly, how could they win their support? And without that support, the government was doomed.

As 1970 ended, there was still no reform. Since America's first involvement in Vietnam, only the names of the government leaders had changed. The government itself remained as corrupt as ever.

Problems with Vietnamization

The effectiveness of Vietnamization was tested in February 1971. That's when the South Vietnamese army pushed into neighboring Laos. Their purpose was to disrupt North Vietnam's supply route. This road was called "Ho Chi Minh Trail." It stretched from Hanoi to South Vietnam and Cambodia.

In Laos, the South Vietnamese would be on their own. Congress wouldn't permit American troops to fight outside Vietnam. But America was providing some support. To back up the South Vietnamese, U.S. forces would be pounding the area with artillery shells and bombs.

Reports were optimistic at first. But after five weeks, hope dimmed. The fighting in Laos was some of the bloodiest of the war. And the South Vietnamese were in retreat.

The operation ended in early April. The South Vietnamese reported 25% casualties, although others claimed the losses went as high as 50%. Vietnamization didn't seem to be working.

In October, American hopes suffered another setback. President Thieu won the South Vietnamese presidential election in a landslide. But he was the only person allowed to run. For politics in South Vietnam, it was business as usual. American forces ended the year with a five-day bombing attack on North Vietnam.

In March 1972, the North Vietnamese stormed through the demilitarized zone. By May 1, they'd captured the city of Quang Tri. A week later, President Nixon ordered the mining of Haiphong Harbor and other ports in North Vietnam.

Whether Vietnamization was working or not, the Americans were pulling out. In August, America withdrew its last ground troops.

Congress wouldn't permit American ground troops to fight outside of Vietnam.

In late October, Secretary of State Henry Kissinger made an announcement. He said that peace was almost at hand. The American elections were almost at hand, too. Some people felt that Kissinger was playing politics. At any rate, the peace talks fell through. In December, they started up again, only to fall apart once more.

Again, President Nixon ended the year with bombing attacks on North Vietnam. This time, B-25s bombed military and civilian targets in Hanoi and Haiphong. The raids were costly for America. The administration claimed that 15 of the B-25s were lost. But other sources said losses were closer to 35.

One thing was perfectly clear. The bombing attacks diminished U.S. prestige in the world. Both friends and foes called the raids unnecessary and barbaric. ■

Massacre at My Lai

In mid-March 1968 the young lieutenant was back from the Vietnamese countryside. He'd been leading a "search and destroy" mission. His task force commander called it "well planned, well executed, and successful." But three years later, a military court called it murder.

The young lieutenant's name was William Calley, Jr. The world came to know him as the leader of the My Lai massacre. Calley's platoon had been sent into My Lai village in search of Vietcong. Once there, they rounded up about 40 men, women, and children.

At Ft. Benning, Georgia, Lt. Calley awaited the jury's verdict on the My Lai incident.

Calley told an enlisted man, "You know what to do with them."

The young soldier thought he was supposed to guard the prisoners.

A little later, Calley came back. "How come they're not dead?" he asked. "I want them dead."

Calley and the young soldier were about 20 feet away from the civilians. Standing side by side, they aimed their M-16 rifles at the terrified villagers. Then they began to fire.

The massacre had begun.

Before the day was over, the village lay in ruins. More than 500 of its people were dead. Some of those had been shot, some bayoneted, some beaten to death. Calley's troops had also raped a number of women and children.

The detailed facts of the massacre weren't put in any reports. But unofficial word of it leaked out. Officially, though, it never happened. A congressional subcommittee later concluded that there had been a cover-up. No one was ever convicted of it however.

A year later, Vietnam veteran Ron Ridenhour did some investigating. He'd learned about My Lai when he was in Vietnam. Through scraps of information, he put the story together. His digging brought about a government investigation.

Orders From Above

Lt. Calley was charged with 102 murders. During his trial he didn't blame the men under him. He did say he'd been acting under orders from Captain Ernest Medina. Medina, his company commander, denied that. He also denied ever seeing the victims of My Lai.

At the trial's end, Calley was found guilty of 22 murders. He was sentenced to life in prison. But five months later, his sentence was reduced to 20 years. That meant he could be paroled in about 6 years.

Many people thought the trial was unfair. Some doves felt that the whole war was criminal. They said Calley was just a scapegoat. Some hawks thought Calley hadn't done anything wrong. They claimed that he was just doing his duty.

One soldier under Calley thought the slaughter was bound to happen. He felt it was the logical result of the war in Vietnam.

"The people didn't know what they were dying for," he said. "And the guys didn't know why they were shooting them." ■

In Paris, in January 1973, the United States, South Vietnam, North Vietnam, and the Vietcong signed an agreement for ending the war.

Cease-Fire Signed, American Troops Leave Vietnam

Secretary of State William P. Rogers was getting writer's cramp. He'd just signed his name 62 times. But it had been worth it. After 12 long years, America was finally getting out of Vietnam. The document he'd just signed made it official. It was called the "Agreement on Ending the War and Restoring Peace in Vietnam."

None of the four signers of the document was absolutely happy with the treaty. Still, on January 27, 1973,

they'd all accomplished something. A cease-fire was to go into effect the next day. The North and South Vietnamese armies would hold onto the territory they had.

The United States agreed to withdraw all its military forces from Vietnam. That would be done within 60 days. And all prisoners of war would be returned within 60 days. The United States also agreed to talk about payments to North Vietnam. The bombing raids there had caused

terrible property damage.

The POW release program quickly got under way. In the first wave, 142 Americans were released at a Hanoi airport. By the middle of February, 20 more had landed on American soil. In all, a total of 562 American POWs were released by the Communists. Some 1,300 were still listed as MIA—missing in action. Most of them were believed dead.

There were still rumors that the Communists had secret POW camps.

Some people thought they were holding Americans there as bargaining chips.

On March 29, 1973, the last American troops left South Vietnam. About 8,500 civilians remained. Most were technicians. They stayed on to

As the fighting continued, South Vietnam's army began to fall apart.

help the South Vietnamese troops.

American involvement in Vietnam was at an end. However, Nixon's bombing of Cambodia still continued. But that was being challenged in Congress.

In May, the House voted to cut off funds. But the House vote

wouldn't become law until the Senate approved it. In the meantime, Nixon stepped up the raids. Then finally, the Senate acted. On August 15, the bombing stopped.

America's direct involvement in the war in Southeast Asia was over.

A Government Crumbles

The cease-fire had looked good on paper, but the fighting between the South and the North continued. Each side blamed the other for skirmishes in contested areas.

After a year of such fighting, President Thieu spoke out. The peace treaty had said everyone could keep the positions they held at the cease-fire. But he found that unworkable. There'd be no peace, he said, "as long as the North Vietnamese stay in the South." Until they withdrew, he wouldn't hold elections.

As the fighting continued, South Vietnam's army began to fall apart.

By March of 1975, the Communists controlled Darlac, Pleiku, and Kontum provinces. And they were approaching Saigon.

Finally, on April 21, Thieu resigned. By then, the Communists had surrounded the capital city. South Vietnamese leaders then appointed Duong Van Minh as president.

As the Communists closed in on Saigon, the remaining Americans were forced to evacuate the city. Emergency helicopters took them to ships waiting off the coast. Thousands of South Vietnamese who feared the Communist takeover tried to join the Americans. There were scenes of chaos as people tried to force their way onto overcrowded helicopters.

Finally, on April 30, President Minh surrendered unconditionally to the Communists. Vietnam was now under complete Communist control. ∎

People escaping from Nha Trang in April 1975 fought for airplane space. Soon after this plane left, Communist troops overran the city.

From the Golan Heights, the Israelis fired on enemy Syrian forces in 1973.

Arabs Surprise Israel with Major Attack

The attacks came on October 6, 1973. It was Yom Kippur—the Day of Atonement. It was the holiest day of the Jewish calendar.

The Israelis were caught unprepared. Egyptian forces struck from the south. They came in across the Suez Canal. In the north, the Syrians attacked. Their forces pushed into the Israeli-held Golan Heights.

October 6 fell in the middle of Ramadan, a holy season for Moslems. That added an element of surprise to the Arab attacks. But that

wasn't why they caught Israel off guard. Basically, the Israeli defense system had relaxed.

In the Six-Day War of 1967, Israel had achieved a stunning victory. The Israelis had expanded their territory in two directions. In the west, they'd seized the Sinai Peninsula. And their border with Egypt was now the Suez Canal. In the north, they'd taken the Golan Heights, pushing into Syrian territory.

The Israelis felt proud of their 1967 victory. But unfortunately for

them, that pride gave way to overconfidence. In 1967 the Israeli Army was disciplined. By late 1973, however, the discipline had grown lax.

When the Yom Kippur War came in 1973, the Israeli reserve forces were disorganized. Their equipment hadn't been properly maintained. Some of their vehicles wouldn't start. Soldiers went into battle without the proper clothing and equipment.

In 1967 the air force and armored corps had brought the Israelis success. The Israeli general

16

staff felt it would do so in the future. As a result, planes and tanks were emphasized instead of the foot soldier. Israel's infantry received second-class attention.

If the 1967 victory had led Israel into overconfidence, it had made the Egyptians train all the harder. The defeat had been very bitter for them. They'd lost territory and they'd been humiliated. They wanted revenge.

The Israelis hadn't considered that factor fully enough. To Israeli thinking, Egypt and Syria would be crazy to risk war: Israeli air power was too strong.

In September and early October 1973, though, there were danger signs for Israel. Syrian troops were conducting large training exercises on Israel's eastern border. Egypt was doing the same along the Suez Canal in the west. Still, the Israelis seemed to downplay the importance of those actions.

Egypt's leader Anwar Sadat had been talking about war for some time. He'd made threats and boasts since early 1972. But the Israelis thought it was all talk.

Israelis Not Ready

Not until the night before Yom Kippur did the Israelis take action. By then the evidence was overwhelming. The Egyptians and Syrians were ready for war. But the Israeli army only called a grade "C" alert. That was basically just a warning to stand by.

Then at 4 A.M., October 6, Israeli chief of staff Elazar was wakened. Israeli and American intelligence had overheard a message. The final war preparations were being made.

Supposedly, the attack would come at 6 P.M.

At 8 A.M. Elazar and General Dayan met with Prime Minister Golda Meir. Elazar wanted authority to attack the Arabs before they attacked. But Prime Minister Meir turned him down. She said that such an attack would cause diplomatic problems. Israel would be seen as the aggressor. That could result in retaliation from other countries.

Israel would have to wait for the attack. It would have to rely on its defenses to hold back the Arab tide. Tank commanders in the north and south were alerted. They were told the attack would begin at 6 P.M. But they weren't allowed to move into position. It was now known that war was coming. But for diplomatic purposes, it was important that Israel not provoke it.   ⇨

Israeli troops and armored vehicles moved into the Sinai Desert during the 1973 Arab-Israeli conflict.

The attack came early. At 2 P.M. a barrage of bombs and shells exploded along Israel's borders. In the north, Syrian troops in helicopters attacked the Golan Heights. They captured Israel's radar station on top of Mount Hermon.

The artillery attack went on for almost an hour. Then Syrian tanks came pushing through. There were two armored divisions, about 800 tanks. Three infantry divisions followed in armored personnel carriers. Israel's planes were battered by conventional antiaircraft fire and SAM rockets.

In the south, Egyptian planes attacked Israeli bases and radar stations. Heavy artillery fire struck along the east side of the Suez Canal. At the peak of the attack, 8,000 Egyptian infantry crossed the canal. They were carried by fast, fiberglass boats. By nightfall the Egyptians had established themselves on the east bank. Some of their troops had advanced three miles beyond that position.

The two-pronged attack was a great success for the Arabs. Not only had they taken territory—they'd proved something. Israelis weren't supermen. And Arabs weren't military misfits.

The Egyptian chief of staff announced, "The war has retrieved Arab honor. Even if we will be defeated now, no one can say that the Egyptian soldier is not a superior fighter."

The Arabs proved that the Israelis weren't supermen.

By October 10 the Israelis were recovering. They concentrated armor and air support on the Syrian invaders. Soon they pushed them back to the 1967 cease-fire lines.

By the eleventh, they were ready for an all-out counterattack on the Egyptians. And by October 19, the Israelis had pushed across the Suez Canal. They had also trapped Egypt's Third Army on the Sinai Peninsula.

Israel was now in a position to crush Egypt. But America and Russia wouldn't permit it. While America was a strong ally of Israel, Russia had been backing the Arabs. Total defeat would be embarrassing to them as well as to Egypt. And America felt it would upset the balance of power in the Middle East. Israel agreed not to press deeper into Egypt.

By late October a cease-fire was in effect. On November 11 an agreement was formally signed by both sides.

Hostilities with Syria continued into 1974. Finally, U.S. secretary of state Henry Kissinger was called in to negotiate. On May 17, 1974, a cease-fire agreement was reached.

Israel had won another victory—but a very costly one. There would be major shake-ups in the armed forces and the government. Many questions would be asked.

The Israelis had fought four major wars in their short history. When would the next one come? Would they be ready? Would they ever know peace? ■

During the Yom Kippur War, Israeli troops pushed into Syria.

Military Overthrows Chile's President

Three times, Salvador Allende had run for president of Chile. Three times he had lost. Then in September 1970, he ran again. He was backed by the Socialists, Communists, Radicals, and some Christian Democrats. This time he won. He received about 36% of the votes. That was more than any of the other candidates. His victory was confirmed by Chile's congress.

His swearing in that November made big news around the world. He was the first Marxist to be democratically elected to head a Western country.

Born in 1908, Allende grew up in a middle-class family. After finishing medical school, he helped found Chile's Socialist party. Between 1937 and 1970 he was active in Chile's government. He was elected to Chile's senate four times.

Allende promised to take Chile "down the road to socialism."

After his election as president, he set out to keep his campaign promises. For one thing, he tried to nationalize the economy. Some privately owned businesses were taken over by the government. He also formed diplomatic ties with some Communist countries. Soon after his election, Chile recognized Cuba and China.

Allende promised to take Chile "down the road to socialism." But, he added, he'd do it in the "framework of the constitution."

During his presidency, relations with the United States became strained. The main causes were his socialism and his treatment of American companies. In September 1971, the Chilean government took over copper mines owned by two U.S. companies. Payment of $774 million was proposed. But Allende said he wouldn't pay the Americans anything. He charged that the companies had made "excess profits" for 16 years.

Major Economic Problems

Allende's plans for a Socialist economy didn't go well. Inflation soared. He faced strong opposition from the middle class. In October 1972, there were strikes across the country. Allende declared a state of emergency in 20 of Chile's 25 provinces. But the situation grew worse.

In September 1973, his government was overthrown by military leaders. During the fighting, some 2,700 Chileans were killed. The new government leaders said that Allende had killed himself just before the armed forces captured the capital. For 46 years Chile had been ruled by a civilian government. Now the new president was army general Augusto Pinochet.

In 1974 it was revealed that the United States was involved in Allende's overthrow. Throughout his presidency, the CIA had been working to "destabilize" Chile's government. With Pinochet in power, the United States expected a more favorable and "friendlier" government to rule Chile. And as the decade progressed, those expectations seemed to be coming true. ∎

Chilean president Salvador Allende was ousted by military leaders in 1973.

A Beirut shopping area was burned and bombed as the civil war continued in 1975.

Civil War in Lebanon

Bombs and Bullets in Beirut

Beirut, Lebanon's capital, was one of the most beautiful cities in the world. For centuries it was a cultural and educational center. Some people called it the "Paris of the Middle East."

In 1975 Beirut was a sophisticated, modern city. High-rise apartments, hotels, and businesses flourished everywhere. It was a time of progress and hope.

That ended when civil war began. A violent incident in April 1975 triggered the war. But some of its causes could be traced back at least 30 years.

Trouble began to develop when the French left Lebanon in 1946. Christians in the minority held most of the government's power. The more numerous Moslems resented that. Then, with the partition of Palestine in 1948, the problem worsened. Palestinian refugees came to Lebanon. The Moslem majority grew greater. But the power stayed in Christian hands.

In the early 1970s, events in neighboring Jordan caused more problems. Jordan's King Hussein didn't want the Palestine Liberation Organization (PLO) there. After his

troops drove them out, many moved to Lebanon. There they settled with other Palestinian refugees in tent camps.

The new refugees created more tension in an already tense situation.

In its new home, the PLO began recruiting. The organization drew many unemployed young men from the Palestinian camps. Soon, they were raiding Israeli villages across the border.

Israel answered back with aerial bombings of the refugee camps. And the PLO commandos also began fighting Lebanese government forces, which were mostly made up of Christians. But it wasn't just troops that were affected. Civilians were dying in the bombings and the fighting as well.

Soon a number of militias sprang up, both Moslem and Christian. They were actually private armies. Before long, they began to fight each other.

The delicate situation was aggravated by yet a new development. All over the Middle East, Moslems were becoming more conservative. Some of them hoped their

Everyday, violence disrupted the life of downtown Beirut.

faith—called Islam—would unite the Arab world. As they moved closer to a fundamental form of Islam, they moved further away from the Christians.

Christians Against Moslems

Lebanon was a westernized country with ties to Christian Europe. Many Moslems thought that was what stood in the way of a united Arab Middle East. So the Christian majority in Lebanon's government came under attack. Moslem nations began to put pressure on the Lebanese government.

Fights between Christian and Moslem militias increased.

On April 13, 1975, militiamen attacked a busload of Palestinians. Many Palestinians were killed. The attackers were Christian Maronites. They were from the major Christian sect in Lebanon.

Soon fighting engulfed the city. On one side were PLO forces and Moslem militias. On the other side were government forces and Christian militias. In the middle, as in most civil wars, were the civilians.

Everyday, bombs and bullets disrupted the life of downtown Beirut. Much of the beautiful city was destroyed.

The fighting went on for 18 months. Then in late 1976, Saudi Arabia led other Arab nations in arranging peace. Syria provided a peace-keeping force of 30,000 men. By the end of the year, the civil war was over.

The fighting had taken a terrible toll. Some 60,000 people had been killed. And about $5 billion in property had been destroyed.

The peace was an uneasy one. The root problems that had started the war had not been solved. The Lebanese could only hope that a solution would come. In the meantime they prayed that another spark would not ignite the blaze again. ■

Beirut residents examine the effects of war on the commercial district.

900 Die in Mass Suicide in Guyana

"Everyone has to die!" shouted cult leader Jim Jones. Apparently, his large crowd of listeners agreed with him. The Jonestown massacre took place on November 18, 1978. When it was over, 909 people had killed themselves.

James Warren Jones was born in Indiana in 1931. He never attended theology school, but he wanted to be a minister. So he began serving as one when he was in his early 20s. A white man, he strongly supported racial integration. In 1955 he opened the integrated Community Unity Church in Indianapolis, Indiana. Later, he changed the name to the People's Temple.

In 1964, Jones was ordained by the Disciples of Christ. His own church, though, was far removed from traditional Christianity. His followers called him "Dad." And they did what he told them. Those who opposed him were beaten in public.

He moved his church—and the members of the People's Temple—to Ukiah, California, in 1965. In 1971 he moved to San Francisco.

Over the years, his behavior grew more and more extreme. He claimed he could cure diseases by faith. He chose mistresses from the members of his church. He told his followers to turn all their money over to him. And he began to depend on drugs.

Meanwhile, he became active in San Francisco politics. For a time he even served on the city's housing commission.

Then in 1976, his strange habits were exposed in a magazine article. He quickly moved his church to Guyana in South America. Almost 1,000 followers, most of them black, went with him. There, in a jungle, they set up the community of Jonestown.

Little was heard of the cult until November 1978. Then, Leo Ryan, a congressman from Northern California, visited Jonestown. He was investigating reports that some Californians were being held there against their will. Several defectors asked Ryan to take them away from Jonestown. But as they headed for their airplane, shots rang out. Ryan, a defector, and three journalists were killed by Jones's supporters.

> ## How could hundreds of people commit suicide on the orders of a single man?

Back at the temple, Jones announced that everyone should die. His followers were ready. They'd been practicing for a mass suicide for months. Most of them willingly drank soft drinks laced with cyanide. Many who refused were injected with poison. Others were shot. A few escaped into the jungle. Jones himself died from a bullet wound.

When the world learned of the tragedy at Jonestown, many people were stunned. How could hundreds of people commit suicide on the orders of a single man? But a more pointed question might have been, how could those hundreds of people have believed in a madman like Jim Jones in the first place? ∎

The world was shocked by the People's Temple massacre at Jonestown, Guyana, in 1978. Here, hundreds of dead bodies lie near the community hall.

Anastasio Somoza Debayle, the last of his family to rule Nicaragua.

Somoza's National Guard searched door-to-door for rebels in mid-1979.

Dictatorship in Nicaragua

One Family's Tyranny Comes to an End

For the Somoza family, Nicaragua was a paradise. They'd ruled the Central American country since 1936. Through the years they'd acquired enormous wealth.

Anastasio Somoza was the first member of his family to rule Nicaragua. But even before becoming president, he wielded great power. He'd been head of the National Guard. In Nicaragua, the National Guard was like the country's police force.

Even then, Somoza was hated by many Nicaraguans. He'd been behind the murder of the rebel hero Augusto César Sandino.

In the years ahead, the Somoza family kept control of the National Guard. They also controlled the president, even when he wasn't a family member.

The Somozas maintained close ties with the United States. They offered America two benefits. First, they supported U.S. policies in Central America. Second, they kept Nicaragua stable.

The cost of those benefits came as a loss of freedom to most Nicaraguans. But that didn't concern the Somozas. They had the support of the United States. They could rule Nicaragua as though they owned it. They were absolute dictators.

> The Somozas could rule Nicaragua as though they owned it. They were absolute dictators.

The rich people who owned most of the farmland grew richer. The peasants grew poorer. They were forced off their small farms and into city slums.

During the family's long rule, there were several attempts to overthrow them. But with the National Guard, the Somozas suppressed any opposition.

In 1967 Anastasio Somoza Debayle, son of the first Somoza to rule, came to power. He continued the dictatorship. The gap between the very rich and the very poor grew even wider. More civil liberties were taken from the people.

Finally, during the 1970s, a new rebel force rose up. They called themselves "Sandinistas." They were named for Sandino, the rebel that Anastasio Somoza had assassinated.

Somoza called on his National Guard to wipe out the rebels. They had done that three times before—in 1954, 1959, and 1967. This time they failed.

On July 19, 1979, President Somoza fled to Miami, Florida. Nicaragua no longer belonged to the Somozas. The Sandinistas had overthrown the government. ∎

The Sandinistas Take Control

The Sandinistas' victory caused mixed feelings, particularly in the United States. For one thing, no one knew for sure who the Sandinistas were.

Many people thought they were Communists. After all, their revolution had been supported by Cuba, a Communist country. On the other hand, it had also been supported by non-Communist Mexico.

In fact, the Sandinistas included people with a variety of political ideas. There were communists and there were capitalists. What united them all was hatred of the Somoza dictatorship.

Even the United States had grown sick of the Somoza family's abuses. During the late '70s, America had finally withdrawn support for the Somoza government. This was demonstrated by the U.S. refusal to send arms to the Nicaraguan National Guard.

Earthquake, Then Civil War

Unrest in Nicaragua had grown intense after the 1972 earthquake in Managua, the capital. Relief money was sent from the United States and the United Nations. But the Somozas used it more for themselves than for helping the country.

By 1978 the unrest had become an outright civil war. Antigovernment rebels fought National Guard forces controlled by Somoza, and backed by many of the wealthy landowners.

During the struggle, the rebels formed the National Sandinista Liberation Front. In short, they called themselves Sandinistas. Their support among the general population grew stronger. There were massive strikes and protests. Some were even supported by the country's leading businessmen. Finally, in July 1979, Somoza gave up power and fled the country.

Once they had overthrown the Somozas, the Sandinistas had several tasks ahead of them. They had to put together a working government. And they had to remain militarily strong. There were still strong pro-Somoza forces who were actively opposing them.

Throughout the 1960s, Nicaraguans had been following events in Cuba. The Cubans had overthrown a dictator who was much like Somoza. Then they'd set up a Communist government.

Many Nicaraguans opposed to the Somozas were capitalists. They wanted free elections and a just government. They didn't want communism. Still, they were willing to work with Communists to overthrow the Somozas.

But problems arose immediately after the overthrow. The Sandinista leaders promised there would be elections, but not until 1984. Until then, they said, they would control the country.

Many supporters of the revolution were wary. It sounded to them like another dictatorship had come to power. Several leaders withdrew from the government.

As 1979 came to a close, the Sandinistas held the power in Nicaragua. But no one knew how long—or at what cost—that power would remain with them. ∎

Nicaraguans prepare to fight members of Somoza's National Guard in the city of Masaya.

The leader of the shah's opposition was Ayatollah Khomeini. Here, his supporters jam the streets of Tehran, Iran, in February 1979.

Islamic Revolution Overthrows Shah of Iran

In 1953 Shah Mohammad Reza Pahlavi assumed power in Iran. Because America had supported him, he saw to it that Iran became a close U.S. ally.

For some time, Western businesses had been kept out of Iran. But with Pahlavi in control, the doors to Iran were reopened. He encouraged westerners to return.

Soon, British, American, Dutch, and French oil companies formed an organization. Working as a unit, they undertook oil production. Profits were split equally between the organization and Iran.

The shah then began to modernize his country. A 7-year plan was put into effect. Oil revenues paid for most of the improvements. But America and other countries also contributed.

Overall, the shah improved economic conditions in Iran. He launched a literacy program. He brought about land reform and increased civil rights for women.

The shah's policies met strong opposition, however. Much of it came from the mullahs, the Moslem clergy. They were opposed to modernization. They said it went against their religion.

Many other people were op-posed to the unequal sharing of oil wealth. It was true that the shah had improved economic conditions somewhat. But many people still lived in poverty. The shah, on the other hand, was fabulously wealthy. And so were many members of the upper class.

Opposition also came from university students. They thought the shah should allow more political freedom.

The shah dealt with all opposition severely. Savak, his secret police organization, was widely feared and hated. Its agents were brutal and cruel. Thousands of ⇨

people were unjustly imprisoned and even murdered.

One man who spoke out against the shah was Ruhollah Khomeini. A religious leader, he was known by the Islamic title "ayatollah."

To silence him the shah put him in prison. In 1964 he exiled Khomeini to Iraq. Later, he moved to Paris.

From there Khomeini directed a movement to overthrow the shah. The ayatollah's taped speeches were smuggled into Iran. Other religious leaders played them to their followers.

In October 1978 Khomeini arranged a general strike in Iran. More strikes and riots followed. Finally, opposition to the shah grew too great. On January 16, 1979, he was forced to flee Iran.

Ayatollah Khomeini's revolution had succeeded.

Islamic Republic of Iran

Two weeks after the shah fled, Ayatollah Khomeini returned in triumph. His taped sermons had inspired the revolution. Because of his imprisonment and exile, he had become a martyr. The streets were packed with supporters upon his return. They welcomed him home with huge rallies.

Under Khomeini's direction, the new Islamic Republic of Iran was established. Mehdi Bazargan was named premier. He had no real power, however. The power was in the hands of the Islamic Revolutionary Council. And the council was in the hands of Ayatollah Khomeini.

The shah dealt with all opposition severely.

Although Khomeini took no political office, he still was in total control. He acted as judge when arguments arose among rival groups. He was skilled at playing off one side against another. His loyal followers, mostly peasants, controlled parliament.

Khomeini's goal was to make Iran a strict Islamic state. Religious law was to become the law of the land. And no important policy decisions could be made without his approval.

Under Khomeini's direction the council stopped the "westernization" of Iran. Advances in civil rights for women were reversed.

The shah's secret police had killed many people. Now many of its members who hadn't escaped Iran were themselves caught and killed. And they weren't the only ones. Many political trials were held. Many death sentences were passed. Within days of the trials, the sentences were carried out.

Amin Abbas Hoveida had been Iran's premier for 13 years. A few months after the revolution, he was executed.

In December 1979 a new constitution was adopted. Under its terms, a religious leader would supervise Iran's political leaders. His title would be Faghi, meaning guide.

The first Faghi appointed was Ayatollah Khomeini. It was a lifetime appointment. ■

Ayatollah Khomeini greets followers from a window after returning to Iran from 15 years in exile.

Demonstrators at the United States embassy in Iran burn an American flag.

Iranian Students Storm U.S. Embassy, Seize American Hostages

As the Islamic revolution took hold in Iran, anti-American feelings flared. After all, the revolutionaries said, America had supported the shah for years. Even now, he was being given shelter in the United States.

It was true that the shah was in an American hospital. He was being treated for cancer. The Carter administration said there was nothing political behind it. He was allowed in the country purely as a humanitarian consideration.

But the Iranians couldn't accept that. To them the shah was a criminal. He was guilty of torturing and killing Iranians. He had also taken millions—maybe billions—of dollars out of Iran. That money, they said, belonged to the Iranian people.

Finally, on November 4, 1979, the Iranians struck at Americans. About 500 militant students attacked the American embassy in Iran's capital, Tehran. They captured 62 Americans and held them hostage.

America was shocked and humiliated.

The militants said they would hold the hostages until certain conditions were met. Mainly, they wanted the shah returned for trial in Iran. They also wanted the money the shah took from Iran. If that didn't happen, they said, they'd put the Americans on trial. If they were found guilty, they'd be executed.

The hostages were pushed through Tehran's streets. Angry crowds screamed and cursed at them. On the sidelines, Iranian students burned American flags.

The spectacle was shown on television around the world. America was shocked and humiliated.

It was hard to know who was in charge. Did these students act on their own? Were they prompted by the Islamic Republic?

Ayatollah Khomeini knew the answers. But he wouldn't supply them. He seemed to be too busy enjoying America's predicament. As 1979 came to an end, the crisis was still unresolved. And no one knew how long the ordeal would last. ∎

National Guard troops advance up a hill at Kent State, moments before the deadly assault on students.

National Guard Troops Kill Student Protesters

President Nixon's announcement on April 30, 1970, surprised most Americans. On the campaign trail in 1968, he had promised to wind down American involvement in the Vietnam War. Now he was expanding it!

Nixon had ordered 30,000 American troops to go into neighboring Cambodia. They were to destroy Communist bases and supplies there. The action was taken, Nixon said, to stop the North Vietnamese from using these bases in the Vietnam War.

The Nixon administration called the action an "incursion." But to many Americans, it looked a lot like an invasion.

At college campuses across the country, students began to protest the action. One such campus was at Kent State University in Ohio.

Soon after the U.S. troops moved into Cambodia, troops moved onto the Kent State campus. These troops belonged to the Ohio National Guard. They'd been sent by Ohio's governor, James Rhodes, to halt the demonstrations. But their actions had the opposite effect. The protest grew more intense.

On May 4 the armed guardsmen went out of control. They fired on the unarmed students, killing four and wounding nine others.

The nation was shocked. College students were gunned down in foreign dictatorships. But how could it happen in America?

It was a very disturbing question, and within two weeks it was raised again.

In Mississippi, the National Guard and police went on a deadly shooting spree. The attack took place at all-black Jackson State College.

Following two days of protests, police and National Guard troops were called to the campus. On the night of May 14, they lined up across from a student dormitory. Just after midnight, someone said there was a sniper in the dormitory. The situation grew even more tense.

Suddenly, the police and National Guard began to fire their weapons. In a half-minute barrage, they fired shotguns, rifles, and machine guns. When they were finished, two students lay dead.

The events at Kent State and Jackson State presented a frightening picture. Those assigned to protect the public had suddenly turned against it. Equally frightening were the cover-ups that followed.

In Kent, Ohio, a grand jury investigated the incident. They decided not to charge the guardsmen who killed the students. Instead, they indicted 25 other people. Among them was the president of Kent State's student body. Their reasoning was that the students brought their deaths upon themselves.

Robert White, president of Kent State, attacked the grand jury's findings. He said their judgment was inaccurate and an attack on all free universities.

A grand jury in Jackson investigated the killings there. They used the same reasoning as the grand jury in Ohio.

They said that students take risks when they engage in civil disorder and riots. "They must expect to be injured or killed when law enforcement officers are required to establish order."

A month after the two incidents, President Nixon appointed William Scranton to head the nine-person Scranton Commission. Their job was to look into the causes of campus unrest.

> Those assigned to protect the public had suddenly turned against it.

The commission members prepared lengthy reports on the Kent State and Jackson State killings. They said the action by the National Guard at Kent State "certainly can't be justified." And they found the deadly attack at Jackson State "an unreasonable, unjustified overreaction."

The commission also attacked the Jackson grand jury's report. Commission members didn't feel students should "expect" injury or death during civil disorders. It was "a view which this commission urges Americans to reject."

The commission's report called on the president to set an example. Because of his influence, only he could calm the angry words of public officials and protesters. Those words, the report said, "have too often helped further divide the country, rather than reunite it."

Vice-President Spiro Agnew disagreed. He said it was unfair to blame President Nixon for student disruptions. He called the report's recommendations, "scapegoating of the most irresponsible sort."

While Americans argued as to who was really to blame for the tragedy, one thing seemed clear. America's college campuses had become a frightening arena of unrest and violence. ∎

In May 1970, a huge crowd gathered near the Washington Monument to protest the Vietnam War and the Kent State killings.

Inmates and Police Clash During Attica Prison Revolt

A military helicopter prepares to drop tear gas into the yard at Attica, New York, during the 1971 riot.

The incident took place on September 8, 1971. Inmates at Attica prison couldn't believe it. Leroy Dewer had hit a guard and had gotten away with it. At least for a while.

Attica is one of New York State's 14 men's prisons. In September 1971, it housed 2,243 inmates. About 54% were black, 37% were white, and 9% were Puerto Rican. The prison was staffed by 380 guards. One of the guards was Puerto Rican and the rest were white.

In the late summer of 1971, Attica was about to explode. In May of that year, Attica inmates had written to corrections commissioner Russell Oswald. They listed 27 changes they thought should be made at the prison. They wanted a new prison doctor. They wanted more than one shower a week. They wanted a baseball diamond in the yard.

The inmates also wanted better and different food—particularly less pork. Many of the black prisoners were Muslims. Their religion didn't allow them to eat pork.

Oswald answered the letter. He agreed that many of the demands were reasonable. However, he said, the prison's budget was tight. It would take time to change things. But on September 9, time ran out at Attica.

Overnight, word had spread through the prison. According to the rumor, Dewer, the prisoner who had hit a guard, hadn't escaped punish-

After the prisoners' uprising, broken furniture and other trash filled the corridors of the cellblocks.

ment after all. Supposedly, he'd been put in solitary confinement and beaten. Those rumors sparked the explosion.

Just before 9 A.M. on September 9, the rebellion began. Guards throughout the prison were overpowered. Ten minutes later, most of Attica was controlled by the inmates. During the takeover, guard William Quinn was badly beaten. He died two days later.

By early afternoon, the inmates had taken 39 civilian hostages. Some of them had been beaten. All had been dressed in inmate clothing and blindfolded. The hostages were brought to one of the prison's four yards. Black Muslims were put on guard, protecting them against inmates who held grudges.

Rockefeller Refuses to Take Part

The leaders of the revolt wanted to speak to public officials. They asked that both Governor Nelson Rockefeller and Commissioner Oswald come to the prison.

Oswald showed up, but Rockefeller sent a representative.

Meanwhile, more than 1,000 New York state troopers and police

were called in. And television and newspaper journalists were let into the prison. The inmates wanted their views known to people outside the walls. Besides Oswald and the press, elected officials and members of black political groups also went in.

The inmates had a number of demands. Most important, they wanted there to be no punishment

---

The state troopers were only to use force to overcome force.

---

for the revolt. But the officials wouldn't agree to that.

The talks went on for several days. The inmates asked again and again that Governor Rockefeller meet with them. But he refused.

Two politicians and two newspaper reporters talked to Rockefeller on the telephone. For 40 minutes they urged him to come to Attica. But again, he refused.

Finally, mediators who had visited the inmates made a plea. They said if Rockefeller didn't personally take part in the negotiations, there would be a massacre. He refused once more.

On September 13, the state troopers and police went into action. Supposedly their instructions were to protect the hostages. They were only to use force to overcome force.

Helicopters dropped tear gas, pepper gas, and mustard gas into the prison. The police and state troopers put on their masks. Moments later, they stormed in. As they did, they began firing their guns.

The attack lasted 15 minutes. The slaughter was terrible. In all, 39 people were killed, including 9 hostages.

Rumors said the inmates had slit some of the hostages' throats during the police attack. That was reported as fact in some newspaper and television reports. In the end, though, it was disproved. All 39 men had been killed by police and state trooper gunfire. In retaking the prison and "restoring order," the authorities had punished the innocent as well as the guilty. ■

The Cold War Thaws as Nixon Visits Red China, Soviet Union

President Richard Nixon had made a career as an anti-Communist. He'd attacked communism every time he'd run for office. He spoke of all Communists as enemies. And he often spoke of his enemies as Communists.

That's why his announcement of July 15, 1971, was so startling. He said he was going to Red China. He'd be making the visit sometime in 1972. It would be, he said, "a journey for peace."

Even before 1971, there had been indications of Nixon's new attitude toward China. In 1969 he'd said that talks with Red China would be of value. And then he'd begun calling it by its proper name. No longer was it "Red China," but the People's Republic of China.

For its part, China was clearly interested in having better relations with America. In 1971 the Chinese hosted an American table tennis team. In addition, they invited a few American journalists to cover the games. That was a major breakthrough. American journalists hadn't

President Richard Nixon is greeted by Chinese Communist party leader Mao Tse-tung in February 1972.

been allowed inside China for more than 20 years.

On April 26, 1971, a Nixon study group came out with an interesting report. The group's report urged that Red China be admitted to the UN. American politicians on the left and the right were confused. Liberals were amazed. Conservatives were enraged. The confusion grew greater with the July 15 announcement. But Nixon had made up his mind.

On February 21, 1972, Nixon arrived in Peking. That same day he met with China's leader, Mao Tse-Tung. The two world leaders spent an hour in secret talks. For the next seven days, Nixon met daily with Chou En-lai. Premier Chou was second in command to Chairman Mao.

Nixon and Mao spent an hour in secret talks.

But there was more to the trip than political talks. Nixon and his wife, Pat, also got the full tourist treatment. They visited the Great Wall. They used chopsticks to eat eight-course dinners. They attended ballet performances at the Great Hall of the People.

At the end of the visit, Nixon suggested a toast to Premier Chou. He spoke of the world role of China and America. He said: "Our two people tonight hold the future of the world in our hands."

Before returning home, Nixon and Chou signed a joint statement calling for a "normalization of relations" between America and China. The cold war between the two countries that had existed for nearly 25 years was beginning to thaw.

Common Ground with the Soviets

The Soviets were unhappy about Nixon's visit to China. They found many of his comments dis-

President Richard Nixon and Soviet leader Leonid Brezhnev sign the Nuclear Arms Limitation treaty in Moscow in 1972.

turbing. China and America held the world's future in their hands? Where did that leave the Soviet Union?

Though the Soviets were unhappy, they weren't about to cancel the summit meeting with Nixon scheduled for May 1972. There was much they hoped to gain from such a meeting.

Soviet leader Leonid Brezhnev had a list of topics to discuss. Among them were pollution, space research, and limitation of strategic nuclear weapons. He was also interested in increased trade with America. The Soviets wanted and needed American technology.

Nixon wanted help in the Vietnam War. Basically, he wanted the Soviets to stop supplying weapons to North Vietnam.

Nixon had made three earlier trips to the Soviet Union. One he made as vice president, during the 1950s. The next two were made as a private citizen.

On his presidential visit, he spent little time sightseeing. For a week, he met daily with Brezhnev and his advisers.

It was a successful trip. America and the Sovet Union agreed to work together on space projects. They'd also work together on problems of soil, water, and air pollution.

Their agreement on strategic nuclear arms was the most important. The discussions were intense, but they paid off in a remarkable agreement. It was probably the most significant one since World War II. It limited the deployment of defensive

missiles. It also said that no more attack missiles could be made for five years.

The agreement didn't eliminate the threat of war. But it kept it from growing worse. Considering the state of the world, that was good news indeed.

Reelection Landslide

Nixon's two major trips abroad turned out to be great successes at home, as well. By the fall of 1972, Nixon's popularity at home was quite high. Many people forgot the "lingering" problem of Vietnam and Nixon's expansion of the war into Cambodia in 1970. Now he seemed to have a new image—"peacemaker."

In November, Nixon defeated his Democratic rival George McGovern in a landslide. McGovern had campaigned on a strong antiwar platform. He had also called Nixon's administration the most "corrupt in U.S. history."

McGovern cited a break-in at Democratic National Headquarters in June 1972 as just one example of the administration's "shady" activities. But the Democrats had no evidence that anyone in the White House had authorized a spying activity at their party headquarters. McGovern's charge had no effect at all on the voters in November.

Three months after the election however, the break-in would surface as a harmless-sounding nine letter word that would unravel a presidency—Watergate. ∎

The Scandal that Shamed a Nation

Watergate: Act I

A "Third-Rate Burglary"

Security guard Frank Will worked at the Washington, D.C., building complex called Watergate. During the early hours of June 17, 1972, he noticed something strange. The latches on two basement doors were taped open. He removed the tape and continued on his rounds.

When he came by again at 1:52 A.M. he saw that the tape was back. So he went to a telephone and called the police.

Shortly after that, the police arrested five men in a sixth floor office. It was the headquarters of the Democratic National Committee.

The five men wore rubber gloves and carried burglar tools. They also carried cameras, electronic bugging equipment, and walkie-talkies. In addition they had with them $5,000 in $100 bills.

All the men gave phony names, but police soon learned who they were. Bernard Barker dealt in Florida real estate. He had once been a Havana policeman. Frank Sturgis was an associate of Barker. Eugenio Martinez worked for Barker. Virgilio Martinez was a Florida locksmith.

The most surprising name was that of James McCord, Jr. He'd

served 20 years with the CIA. Now he was security coordinator for President Richard Nixon's reelection committee. It was called the Committee to Reelect the President, or CRP. The Democrats called it CREEP.

An investigation soon led to two other men: E. Howard Hunt and G. Gordon Liddy. Hunt had also been a CIA man. He'd recently served as a White House consultant. And Liddy was a former FBI agent who was now working as general counsel for CRP.

President Nixon's administration dismissed the importance of the break-in. Press secretary Ron Ziegler called it "a third-rate burglary attempt."

Democratic Senator George McGovern was Nixon's opponent in the upcoming election. During the campaign he tried to make an issue

Necktie flying in the breeze, convicted Watergate burglar James McCord leaves the federal courthouse in Washington. McCord's letter to Judge John Sirica helped expose the Watergate cover-up.

out of the break-in. But the voters didn't seem interested.

Nixon himself said his staff had conducted a complete investigation. He made the results perfectly clear. "No one in this administration, presently employed, was involved in this very bizarre incident."

But if Nixon was satisfied, the press wasn't. Investigative journalists began digging up facts.

For example: Liddy and Hunt had been in the Watergate that night. CRP had taped National Democratic Committee phone conversations. There'd probably been an earlier break-in to plant "bugs"—electronic listening devices.

A Judge Presses for the Truth

The "Watergate 7" went on trial on January 8, 1973. The judge was John Sirica, known to be tough and honest. McCord and Liddy pleaded

> After McCord's letter came out, the veil of secrecy began to lift.

not guilty. Rather than testify, the other five pleaded guilty.

But Sirica didn't let it rest there. "The function of a trial judge is to search for truth," he said. He took an active part in questioning the men.

During the trial, some disturbing facts came out. There was indeed a secret CRP operation. Its purpose was spying and sabotage. And it seemed to be operating out of the White House.

At the end of the trial, both Hunt and Liddy were found guilty. On March 23 Judge Sirica announced the sentences. Liddy had remained silent. He was fined $40,000 and given a 6- to 20-year prison term.

The others got maximum sentences. Sirica hinted that the sentences would be lessened if the men cooperated in future investigations.

James McCord had already

Former attorney general John Mitchell authorized funds from the Nixon Reelection Committee to pay off the Watergate burglars.

agreed to that. In a letter to Sirica, he confessed there'd been a cover-up. He also said that perjury had been committed. The fact was, he said, higher-ups were indeed involved.

After McCord's letter came out, the veil of secrecy began to lift. Jeb Stuart Magruder was the first to confess. He was deputy director of CRP. He said John Mitchell, while attorney general, had approved the break-in. Magruder also tied in President Nixon's counsel, John Dean.

Other details followed quickly. Acting FBI director L. Patrick Gray had destroyed evidence. Herbert Kalmbach, Nixon's private lawyer, had paid people to sabotage the Democrats. In addition, Nixon's top two advisers, H. R. Haldeman and John Ehrlichman, were involved.

By now, Americans were deeply interested in this "third-rate burglary attempt." The Nixon administration was beginning to seem like a Mafia operation. It was time for the president to speak out.

On April 17 he appeared on television. He said he'd accepted the resignations of Haldeman, Ehrlichman, and Dean. He said he'd been unaware of a cover-up, but now he knew.

He took "responsibility" but no blame. The mess, he said, was caused by "people whose zeal exceeded their judgment."

After the broadcast, Nixon spoke to news reporters. "We've had our differences in the past," he said. "And I hope you give me hell every time you think I'm wrong."

He wouldn't have long to wait. ∎

Watergate Committee Chairman Senator Sam Ervin (far right) confers with some of his committee and staff. On the far left are Senators Howard Baker and Lowell Weicker.

Watergate: Act II

The Senate Hearings Expose a Cover-up

Senator Sam J. Ervin, Jr., looked and sounded like a "good old boy." But the North Carolina Democrat's rustic appearance and manner were deceiving. He was considered the Senate's leading constitutional scholar.

Ervin had earned a reputation for fairness. He placed the good of the country above party politics. For those reasons, he was chosen to chair the Senate Watergate Committee hearings.

At age 76, Ervin felt fully prepared to do the job. He called the hearings, "the most important investigation ever entrusted to Congress."

The televised hearings opened on May 17, 1973. The first phase would be an investigation of the Watergate burglary cover-up.

The first major figure to testify was Watergate burglar James McCord. He told of secret meetings with White House intermediary John Caulfield. McCord claimed that he'd

been offered a deal if he kept silent about the break-in. He said Caulfield told him the offer came from the White House.

A few days later, Caulfield verified McCord's testimony. But, he emphasized, President Nixon hadn't made the offer. He said the president's counsel, John Dean had.

Dean warned Nixon that "we have a cancer close to the presidency that is growing."

Day after day, evidence of the cover-up mounted. Herbert Porter, a former Nixon campaign aide, admitted to perjury. He said he'd lied both to the grand jury and at the Watergate burglary trial.

CRP's deputy director Jeb Magruder admitted his role in the cover-up. He also claimed former attorney general John Mitchell had approved money for the break-in. He added that it was a reluctant decision.

Why was that? he was asked.

Magruder answered, "We knew it was illegal, and nothing might come of it."

The nation eagerly awaited the appearance of President Nixon's former counsel John Dean. It was known that he and Nixon had not parted company on the best of terms.

Dean and Nixon advisers John Ehrlichman and H. R. Haldeman had resigned together. Nixon had praised the two advisers. But he'd accepted Dean's resignation without comment.

Dean's testimony took a week. He detailed the involvement of the men closest to the president. And he supplied numerous documents to back up his testimony.

Dean said he'd been assigned to the cover-up. He also said that as the cover-up continued, he warned Nixon about the dangers to the administration. He said he told the president, "We have a cancer within, close to the presidency, that is growing."

Dean also mentioned the first time Nixon had congratulated him on managing the cover-up. The date, he said, was September 15, 1972. That was a shocker. Nixon had publicly claimed that it was much later when he'd learned about the cover-up. Dean's testimony was devastating.

Testifying next, John Mitchell denied he'd approved the break-in. He also said everyone's concern had always been to protect the president.

Butterfield's Bombshell

The high drama of the hearings increased greatly when White House aide Alexander Butterfield testified. During his testimony, he mentioned that the White House had a taping system. All the president's conversations had been tape-recorded.

The news was a bombshell. It meant that Dean's and Nixon's conversations had all been recorded. In theory it could be absolutely determined whether or not Dean was telling the truth.

The problem for the Senate Watergate Committee would be getting the tapes. President Nixon claimed executive privilege. For security reasons, he said, he couldn't release them.

For the moment, the committee would be denied the tapes. But they began legal action to gain their release. They knew the tapes were vital, and they were determined to get them.

Meanwhile, John Ehrlichman testified. He admitted he'd authorized payments to the Watergate burglars. In his opinion it wasn't "hush money." He saw nothing wrong with it. He also said he'd approved covert activities that led to another burglary.

When H. R. Haldeman testified,

there were no surprises at first. He claimed that he didn't know about the cover-up. Then he mentioned that he'd heard some of the tapes. He said that after Dean's testimony, Nixon had let him take some home. But Haldeman hadn't been in public office then. He was a private citizen.

Nixon had said he couldn't release the tapes for security reasons. Chairman Ervin pointed out that Nixon's argument was now weakened.

In mid-August the committee called a recess. The members had

much more work ahead of them. Still, they'd already accomplished a great deal.

The testimony they'd heard laid the groundwork for criminal indictments. Later, Mitchell, Dean, Haldeman, and Ehrlichman would be sentenced to prison terms. And they were only four of many who would be brought down by Watergate.

As the committee took a rest, President Nixon pondered his next move. There seemed little chance he'd be getting any rest for a while. ∎

John Dean's testimony at the Senate Watergate hearings was severely damaging to President Nixon.

A student at Duke University catches up on the Watergate news beneath a sign of the times, in late 1973.

Senator James Eastland, Archibald Cox, and Elliot Richardson (left to right), just before Richardson was confirmed as attorney general in 1973. His first official act was to appoint Cox as Watergate special prosecutor.

Watergate: Act III

Saturday Night Massacre, Talk of Impeachment

The Senate Watergate hearings continued through the spring and summer of 1973. At the same time, a criminal investigation was being conducted by the U.S. Justice Department. But that created a problem.

There already had been testimony of administration cover-ups. What was to prevent more? How could the American people trust Nixon's Justice Department to investigate members of the Nixon administration?

Critics called for a "special prosecutor." They said it should be someone outside the control of the administration. The president finally agreed. He said he had nothing to hide. In late May 1973, Archibald Cox was appointed to be the special prosecutor. Cox was a Harvard Law School professor with a solid reputation. He would report to the attorney general, but otherwise he'd have

complete independence.

Nixon said he'd give Cox his full support. But in October 1973, Cox asked for tapes of White House conversations. Nixon refused to hand them over. Cox persisted.

"I am not a crook," Nixon announced.

On Saturday, October 20, Nixon ordered Attorney General Elliot Richardson to fire Cox. Richardson refused and resigned in protest. Nixon then ordered Deputy Attorney General William Ruckelshaus to fire Cox. He also refused and resigned in protest.

Finally, Nixon turned to the third man in the department, Solici-

tor General Robert H. Bork. Acting as attorney general, Bork fired Cox.

The reaction to the firing was immediate. More than 250,000 telegrams protesting Cox's dismissal flooded the White House. Because of the resignations of Richardson and Ruckelshaus, the press labeled the affair the "Saturday Night Massacre" at the Justice Department.

Eventually, public criticism forced Nixon to appoint a new special prosecutor, Leon Jaworski. But in the meantime, events had reached a turning point. Many people in the country were now beginning to believe that Richard Nixon could not, and should not, continue as president.

In late October, the House Judiciary Committee began an inquiry to determine whether Nixon should be impeached. Impeachment wouldn't mean that the president would be removed from office. It would mean that he'd have to stand trial in the Senate. Then, only if he were convicted would he be removed from office. Conviction would require a two-thirds vote of the Senate.

Only one other president, Andrew Johnson, had ever been impeached. And he'd been found not guilty. That might have been of some encouragement to Nixon. But there was discouraging news ahead.

In November, Republican senator Edward W. Brooke called for Nixon's resignation. Several newspapers also urged him to resign.

Two weeks later Nixon addressed a gathering of newspaper editors in Florida. He maintained his innocence, telling them, "I am not a crook."

As the possibility of impeachment grew stronger, questions arose. No one was sure if there was enough reason to remove Nixon from office.

The House Judiciary Committee lawyers had one opinion. They felt that Nixon didn't have to be guilty of a crime. They said that grave offenses against the public interest were cause enough.

Nixon disagreed. He felt that criminal misconduct had to be proved. On February 24, 1974, he said, "I do not expect to be impeached." Many people felt that was wishful thinking. ∎

Spiro Agnew—A Household Word

Vice-President Spiro Agnew got his job because of what he didn't do. And then he lost it because of what he did do.

Spiro T. Agnew was born in Baltimore, Maryland, in 1918. He attended Baltimore's Johns Hopkins University and the Baltimore Law School.

After service in World War II, he returned to law school. He graduated in 1947 and began practicing law.

In 1957 Agnew was appointed to the Baltimore County zoning board. In 1962 he was elected to the office of county executive.

In 1966 he ran for governor of Maryland against an avowed racist. With the backing of liberals and blacks, Agnew won the election.

In 1968 Agnew supported Nelson Rockefeller for the Republican presidential nomination. When Rockefeller backed out, Agnew switched. He placed Richard Nixon's name in nomination at the convention.

When Nixon chose Agnew as his running mate that year, many people were surprised. Outside of Maryland, Agnew was unknown.

Nixon felt that was an advantage. He had considered other men for the job. But some, such as New York's mayor John Lindsay, were too liberal. Others, such as California's governor Ronald Reagan, were too conservative. Nixon was afraid someone either too liberal or too conservative might offend too many voters around the country.

The unknown Agnew, it was thought, had never done anything to offend anyone. He'd be the perfect candidate. That idea soon proved false.

During the campaign, Agnew predicted that his name would become a household word. It did, but for the wrong reason. He uttered several racial slurs that offended many people. He called a reporter of Japanese ancestry a "fat Jap." He called Americans of Polish decent "Polacks." When asked why he didn't campaign in the ghettos, he offended blacks. "If you've seen one city slum," he said, "you've seem them all."

But despite Agnew's offensive remarks, the Nixon ticket won. During Nixon's first term, Agnew frequently made headlines. He severely criticized antiwar groups and college protesters as unpatriotic. One of his favorite targets was the national media, the "liberal, left-wing" television networks and some newspapers around the country. He accused them of being a "closed fraternity of privileged men" who were quick to criticize the Nixon administration.

Four years later, with Agnew's popularity high among conservatives, Nixon kept him on the ticket. Again, the Nixon team was elected. But Agnew's term in office was cut short.

In 1973 crooked dealings in his past came to light. He was accused of having taken bribes and kickbacks as Maryland's governor. Finally he was charged with federal income tax evasion. In October 1973, he agreed to resign if he didn't have to go to jail. He was fined $10,000 and given three years probation.

As predicted, Spiro Agnew's name had certainly become a household word. But the house had nearly been a jailhouse ∎

Watergate: Act IV
Nixon's Presidency Falls

Throughout the spring of 1974, President Nixon's situation grew worse. Investigators kept uncovering more damaging material.

On July 24 the Supreme Court gave Nixon very bad news. He had been keeping 64 tapes from the special prosecutor. Now the Supreme Court ruled unanimously that he had to turn them over.

Within a week, another blow struck Nixon. The House Judiciary Committee voted three separate articles of impeachment against him. And the committee hadn't even heard what was on the tapes.

As it turned out, the tapes were very damaging. They proved that Nixon had lied about the cover-up. On one tape the president could be heard talking about covering up the break-in six days after it occurred.

On August 4 the president called his closest advisers to Camp David. There he told them what was on the tapes. They were shocked. They realized then that there was no hope

for Nixon's presidency. Several of them advised him to resign.

Nixon also realized how damaging the tapes were. But to the amazement of his advisers, he refused to resign.

The House Judiciary Committee's impeachment vote hadn't been unanimous. On the main charge against Nixon— obstruction of justice—there had been 21 Democratic votes and 6 Republican votes for impeachment. But 11 Republicans on the committee had voted against it.

One of them, Charles Wiggins of California, had strongly backed Nixon. But the evidence on the latest tapes changed even his mind. He realized, finally, that Nixon had taken part in the cover-up.

Wiggins and the ten other Nixon supporters on the committee announced that they thought the president should be impeached.

Yet, with support crumbling all around him, Nixon still wouldn't

resign. All he needed was one-third of the Senate to back him. He thought it was still possible to avoid conviction there.

On August 6 the Republican leadership in the Senate reached a decision. They would ask Senator Barry Goldwater to talk to Nixon. Goldwater was one of the most respected men in the Republican

---

Goldwater summed up the situation for Nixon in one word: "Hopeless."

---

party. But before Goldwater could arrange a meeting, Nixon called him. He invited him and two other Republican leaders to the White House.

They met on August 7. Nixon looked terrible. The recent events had worn him down. The Republicans told him that he didn't stand a

The House Judiciary Committee recommended that President Nixon be impeached on three charges.

chance. It was certain the full House of Representatives would vote to impeach him. And the Senate would vote to convict him. Goldwater summed up the situation in one word: "Hopeless."

Nixon seemed to realize now that he had no choices left. "I just wanted to hear it from you," he said.

He told them that he would soon make a decision. And he assured them it would be in the national interest.

The next evening, August 8, he spoke to the nation on television. As everyone knew by then, it would be his farewell speech. He announced, "I shall resign the presidency effective at noon tomorrow."

Just after noon on August 9, Vice-President Gerald Ford became the new president of the United States.

Ford's inaugural speech was brief and informal. He stressed the need for national unity. He also asked that Americans pray for the Nixon family.

His final words echoed in the hearts of people across the nation. "My fellow Americans," he said, "our long national nightmare is over." ∎

President Nixon says farewell to the White House on August 9, 1974, after being forced out of office.

Woodward and Bernstein: Uncovering the Cover-up

Throughout 1972 and 1973, the names Bob Woodward and Carl Bernstein appeared frequently above stories in the *Washington Post*. When they did, President Richard Nixon and his men usually shuddered.

The two young investigative reporters were assigned to cover the Watergate story. It was through their efforts that many of the details of the Nixon administration's involvement in Watergate became known. For months, they were nearly the only members of the press investigating the story on a daily basis.

Although they came from different political and economic backgrounds, Woodward and Bernstein made an effective team. Early on, they suspected that the break-in was more than just a "third-rate burglary." So they began checking the connections between the burglars and the Nixon reelection committee. Soon the trail began to lead to powerful figures in the administration such as former attorney general John Mitchell and Nixon adviser H. R. Haldeman.

Throughout the early months of the scandal, the administration accused Woodward and Bernstein of "lies" and "political propaganda." Even some other members of the press thought the two reporters were on a "political witch hunt." Fortunately, their paper stood behind them in their investigations.

Woodward and Bernstein got much of their information from a secret source they called "Deep Throat." They never revealed who the person was. But the information they obtained from their source helped them expose many details of the scandal.

After the full story of the cover-up became known, the two reporters were given much credit for their work. They were praised for their efforts by both government officials and their press colleagues.

And because of their reporting, the *Post* received a Pulitzer Prize for its coverage of the entire Watergate scandal. ∎

Washington Post writers Bob Woodward (left) and Carl Bernstein broke the Watergate affair wide open.

Gerald Ford— The Accidental President

Gerald Ford's journey to the White House was accidental. The only votes he ever got came from his Michigan congressional district.

The man who would be the nation's 38th president was born Leslie King in 1913 in Omaha, Nebraska. When he was adopted by his stepfather, he became Gerald Ford. He graduated from the University of Michigan, where he starred in football. Later he went on to graduate from Yale law school.

After service in the Navy, Ford practiced law. In 1948 he was elected to Congress for the first time. Voters in his district liked him. They re-elected him 12 times. In fact, most people liked him. Even his political opponents thought he was a decent man.

In October 1973, Vice-President Spiro Agnew faced a number of criminal charges. As part of a deal to avoid jail, he was forced to resign. That left the vice presidency open. President Nixon was on shaky ground because of Watergate. He needed to find a new vice president— and soon.

Ford seemed like a good replacement. The popular Congressman was acceptable to most Republicans and Democrats. In less than two months he was confirmed as vice president. But he didn't hold the job long. Eight months later, to avoid facing impeachment, President Nixon resigned in disgrace.

As Ford took over from Nixon, he gave words of hope to the country. "Our Constitution works," he said. "Our great republic is a government of laws and not of men."

But those words seemed hollow a month later when he pardoned Nixon. Ford said that the unconditional pardon was "for any offenses he might have committed while in office." Many people thought a deal had been made. They thought Nixon had agreed to resign if Ford would pardon him. Ford denied it, however. He said that he pardoned Nixon to spare the country. A long trial, he felt, would do more harm than good.

But that argument left many people unconvinced.

Ford's term of office was unremarkable. He wasn't able to work effectively with the Democratic majority in Congress. There was widespread unemployment. Prices were rising. All those factors hurt his chances for being elected to another term. The Nixon pardon, though, probably did far more damage.

In 1976 he tried to win the election as president on his own. He lost a very close race to Jimmy Carter. ■

President Gerald Ford shakes hands with Democratic presidential candidate Jimmy Carter before their October 6, 1976, debate.

"I'm Jimmy Carter"

Peanut Farmer with a Goal

Before he began his speeches, the peanut farmer would give a toothy grin. "I'm Jimmy Carter," he'd tell the crowd. "I'm running for president."

At first, many people asked, "Jimmy who?"

But before long the whole country knew. And they found out that he meant business. The former governor of Georgia seemed like an easy-going fellow. But he was dead serious about his goal.

At first many people asked, "Jimmy who?"

In the summer of 1974, he decided he wanted to be president.

And by January 20, 1977, he was.

James Earl Carter, Jr., was born in 1924 in the farming community of Plains, Georgia. He graduated from the U.S. Naval Academy in Annapolis in 1946. His term of service was spent in the submarine program. Afterwards, he returned to Plains and became a successful peanut farmer.

In 1970 he was elected governor of Georgia. After finishing his term in January 1975, he devoted himself full time to seeking the presidency.

Across America, people were attracted to him. After the disgrace of the Nixon administration, Carter seemed like a good and decent man. He spoke of bringing a new broom to Washington. He said he'd "sweep the house of government clean."

Carter said he'd "sweep the house of government clean."

Early in the primaries he took command. He easily won the Democratic nomination. In the election itself he faced the incumbent president, Gerald Ford. When the electoral votes were counted, Carter had 297 to Ford's 240.

Much of Carter's support was a reaction to the Nixon scandals. Ford hadn't been involved in Watergate. But many people resented the unconditional pardon he had given Nixon.

Carter began his presidency graciously. In his inauguration speech, he had kind words for Ford. He gave him credit for keeping the country together after Watergate. He thanked him for all that he had done "to heal our land."

Then, when his speech was over, he unpacked his new broom. He had a lot of housecleaning ahead of him. ■

President Jimmy Carter and Panamanian general Omar Torrijos sign
the treaty that will turn the Panama Canal over to Panama in 1999.

The Carter Years:
Triumphs and Troubles

As Jimmy Carter took office, the country was coming out of a recession. During his campaign, Carter had blamed President Ford for the country's economic problems. Now the Carter administration would try to curb inflation and increase employment.

The promise had helped him in his campaign. But keeping it proved to be impossible. Inflation rose from 4.8% in 1976 to 11% in 1979. The unemployment rate took a very slight drop. And the growing deficit was a major problem. Carter had promised to reduce it, but was unable to. The deficit was closely tied to American dependence on foreign oil.

Carter warned about an energy crisis. He said Americans wasted too much energy and that America's

supply of oil and natural gas was running low. He said the United States would get in trouble if it depended on foreign oil. Americans could be subjected to high prices or a limited supply.

As oil shortages developed in 1977, he spoke to the nation. He said that Americans would have to cut back. He called the effort to save energy, "the moral equivalent of war." He was able to get Congress to approve much of his energy program.

Among other domestic successes, Carter overhauled the civil service system. He also increased funding for education.

His deregulation of the airlines brought about more competition. That meant lower fares for consumers. Carter also pleased en-

vironmentalists by preserving huge areas of wilderness in Alaska.

But he wasn't able to get support for his health-plan proposal. Nor could he bring about reforms in welfare. And though he tried to push a tax-reform program, it went nowhere.

By the end of 1979, Jimmy Carter and his fellow Americans both realized that good intentions weren't enough. Setting goals and achieving them were two different things.

Conservatives Angry

In foreign affairs, Carter experienced some triumphs. Two of them made conservatives angry. First, he persuaded the Senate to ratify a treaty giving control of the Panama Canal to Panama in 20 years. Second, he began full diplomatic relations with China.

For a while he seemed to have made a major arms-control advance. In June 1979 he met with Soviet president Leonid Brezhnev in Vienna. There, they signed the strategic arms limitation treaty (SALT II). This agreement limited the number of nuclear weapon systems the countries could build up. But SALT II faced opposition in the Senate. Then, in December 1979, the Soviets invaded Afghanistan. This was a blow to Carter's peace efforts. From then on, the treaty was as good as dead.

Carter was proudest of his March 1979 foreign policy achievement. In late 1978 he had sponsored Israeli-Egyptian peace talks. They were held at Camp David, Maryland, the president's retreat. There, Egypt's president Sadat and Israel's prime minister Begin met for historic talks.

In March 1979 the "Camp David

Begin said that they should be called the "Jimmy Carter Accords."

Accords" were signed. The agreement called for, among other things, a permanent peace treaty between Egypt and Israel. Both Sadat and Begin gave Carter credit for the arrangements. "They should be called the Jimmy Carter Accords," Begin said.

In November 1979 Carter faced a strange foreign policy problem. Militant students in Iran had seized the U.S. embassy there and taken 62 American diplomats and embassy workers hostage.

The students were protesting America's relationship with the deposed shah of Iran. They made demands of Carter that the United States couldn't meet. As 1979 came to an end, the students still held the hostages. They talked openly of killing them.

The Camp David agreements had given Carter a crowning achievement in foreign policy. But the situation in Iran threatened to develop into the worst crisis of his presidency. ■

President Anwar Sadat, of Egypt, President Jimmy Carter, of the United States, Prime Minister Menachem Begin, of Israel, (left to right) join hands after the signing of the Camp David Accords.

Three Mile Island
Nuclear Crisis in Pennsylvania

Early in 1979, moviegoers flocked to *The China Syndrome*. It was a thriller about a near-disaster at a nuclear power plant. Some critics said it was typical Hollywood nonsense. In the *real* world, it couldn't happen. At nuclear power plants, they said, there were too many safeguards.

But on March 28, 1979, the line between fact and fiction blurred. A major nuclear-reactor accident *did* occur. It happened at the Three Mile Island nuclear reactor near Harrisburg, Pennsylvania.

A nuclear power plant is used to generate electricity. It works something like a coal- or oil-burning power plant.

All three use heat to turn water into steam. The steam powers the turbines in the electricity generators.

Nuclear plants create heat by "splitting" the nuclei of atoms. This splitting, or fission, creates "atomic" energy. In a bomb this process releases the energy in a huge explosion.

In a nuclear plant, the energy is released more slowly. Vast amounts of water are used to control the heat. The plants themselves are huge, filled with miles of pipes. If the cooling system fails, a "meltdown" could occur. Then the atomic fuel could melt through the reactor.

Scientists don't know exactly what would happen after that. But they do know that enormous amounts of energy would be released.

Of course nuclear plants have safety systems with thousands of safety devices. In theory, any problems can be quickly corrected.

But at Three Mile Island, the safety system failed. For a while, there was the possibility of meltdown or a huge explosion. But finally, the problem was brought under control. It turned out that one sticky valve had started the accident. Human and mechanical errors complicated it.

The accident at Three Mile Island offered a lesson: in highly complicated systems, there was still no way to guarantee complete safety. And the world was a much more dangerous place because of that fact. ■

Mechanical and human failures at the nuclear power plant at Three Mile Island, Pennsylvania, alarmed the nation.

The world's first test-tube baby, Louise Brown, with her mother Lesley, a little more than a year after Louise's birth.

Louise Brown—
The World's First Test-Tube Baby

One summer night in 1978, John Brown tried to relax by watching television. He was in a hospital lounge in Bristol, England, waiting anxiously. Lesley, his wife, was upstairs in the maternity ward. There had been some complications. The doctors had decided to perform a Caesarian operation.

John had been told not to worry, that the operation should be routine. Still, he couldn't help worrying. It would be his and Lesley's first child. And that wasn't all. The child would be the first "test-tube" baby in history.

To create human life, a woman's ovum—or egg—must be fertilized. That happens when the female's ovum and the male's sperm combine.

But there was no way a sperm could reach Lesley Brown's ovum. She had a medical condition called "blocked Fallopian tubes." Doctors had told her she could never have a child.

Still, her doctor said, there was one possibility. Scientists had been experimenting with in vitro fertilization. That was a method of combining sperm and ovum outside the body. It had worked with animals. But it had never been tried with humans.

Since Lesley and John wanted a baby very much they decided to try the in vitro method. The term "test-tube baby" wasn't correct. The mixing would actually take place in a petri dish. That was a kind of dish used in laboratories.

First, the doctors surgically removed an ovum from Lesley's body. Then they combined it with John's sperm in the petri dish. The fertilized egg was kept warm for two days. By then it was ready to be implanted in Lesley's womb. About two weeks later, she learned that it had worked. She was pregnant.

As the months passed, the doctors felt all was going well. Still, they wouldn't know for sure until the actual birth. Then on July 25, as John watched television, a doctor interrupted him.

"Congratulations," he said. "You're a father."

Five-pound, twelve-ounce Louise Brown had just come into the world. She was a perfectly healthy baby. The in vitro method had been a great success. And medicine and science had taken another giant leap into the future. ■

High-Tech Explosion Sets Stage for Computer Revolution

Imagine a machine that could perform 5,000 arithmetic operations a second!

In 1946 many people called ENIAC an "electronic brain." It was the first general purpose computer. Built for the army, it was used to help aim large guns. But putting a shell on target was just a beginning. Within 25 years, new generations of computers would help put a man on the moon.

ENIAC had 19,000 separate parts. It was so big it took up most of a large room. But only a handful of scientists could have guessed that much smaller computers were on the way.

The early computers were very expensive. Only governments and large companies could afford to use them. By the end of the 1970s, however, personal computers were widely used in small offices and private homes. More powerful than ENIAC, they were about the size of a suitcase.

The computer revolution was in full gear.

One step in the development of computers came in the early 1970s. In the fifties and sixties, portable calculators were heavy and awkward to carry. Then in 1971, the first "pocket" calculators were mass-produced. As the name suggested, you could carry them in your pocket. By the end of the 1970s, they'd grown even smaller. Some were no bigger than a credit card.

Computers changed the way people handled their money. Banks could now send information electronically. Customers could do their banking by using coded cards. People could even do their banking by telephone, using sound codes.

In 1973 many American stores adopted the Universal Product Code (UPC). Instead of hand stamping the price on items, stores could electronically label the prices in UPCs. Appearing as a small block of narrow black-and-white bars, these codes sped up lines in supermarkets. Now checkers could run items by a laser, a special kind of light. The laser could "read" the cost of each item and then send the information electronically to a computer.

ENIAC was the first fully electronic digital computer. Built in 1946, the huge "adding machine" used bulky vacuum tubes to control its operations.

Steve Jobs (left) and Steve Wozniak shown here with the first Apple computer, built in 1976.

Computer development wasn't just being done by big companies. Enterprising young people were getting into the act on their own.

Electronic Games

In the early 1970s, college student Nolan Bushnell had an idea. Using computer chips, he built an electronic tabletop game based on table tennis. He put one of the games in a restaurant and charged a quarter to play it. It was a great success. So many people tried it, the machine broke from overuse.

Bushnell then started the Atari company to make more game machines. The first game Atari marketed was called PONG. It started a video-game craze that built a multimillion dollar industry.

In 1976 college dropouts Steve Wozniak and Steve Jobs raised $1,300. They used the money to buy computer chips and other electronic components. Then they went to work in a small garage. In six months they'd built a computer. A computer store owner quickly sold it for them. Then he ordered 50 more!

> # Many people began to fear the side effects of the computer revolution.

By the end of 1976, Wozniak and Jobs had sold $200,000 worth of computers. That was just the beginning for Apple Computer Company.

As the decade ended, the influence of computers was being felt everywhere. The computer boom had created many new jobs.

There were drawbacks, however. During the Watergate investigation, the people learned how easily the government could spy on citizens and how efficiently that information could be gathered and stored in computers.

Many people began to fear the side effects of the computer revolution. It seemed that everybody had a number. Those numbers could be used to invade personal privacy. Computer technology could give the government too much control.

Work was made easier by computers. But in the long run, would the bad side effects of them outweigh the good? As the 1970s ended, no one could say. One thing was sure, though. The computer revolution was only beginning. Who could say what astonishing leaps in "high technology" would be made in the 1980s? ∎

A terrorist in a ski mask peeked from the Olympic village apartment where the hostages were being held in 1972.

Tragedy at Munich

Arab Terrorists Murder Israelis at '72 Olympics

People who remember athletic accomplishments at the 1972 Olympics usually think of Mark Spitz. The young American dominated the swimming events, winning an unheard of *seven* gold medals.

However, one episode at the '72 Games in Munich, Germany, overshadowed all other events. It had nothing to do with athletic feats or record-breaking performances. It had to do with violence, political terrorism, and senseless murder.

In the early morning hours of September 5, the Olympic village was awakened by the sounds of gunfire. Eight Arab terrorists had attacked the building housing the Israeli Olympic team. Two Israelis were murdered. Nine more were taken hostage. What could have possibly provoked such an attack?

In Israel, 200 Arab guerrillas were being held in jail. The terrorists wanted them set free. They issued a warning. If their demands weren't met, they'd shoot the Israeli hostages.

The Israeli government said it wouldn't give in to terrorists. No matter what, it wouldn't free the jailed guerrillas.

The terrorists refused to negotiate. That wasn't surprising. They belonged to Black September, one of the most extreme terrorist groups.

Showdown at Airport

When a standoff was reached, the terrorists said they wanted a plane to fly them out of Germany. The German authorities agreed, on the condition that the hostages be set free. Helicopters then flew the terrorists and their hostages to a German airport. But, when the helicopters landed, German sharpshooters began to fire. Five of the eight terrorists were killed. But all nine hostages also died. They'd been murdered by the terrorists as they sat tied and blindfolded in the helicopters.

The Olympic world was in shock. Many nations felt the remainder of the Games should be immediately canceled. They said that the entire spirit of the Olympics had been permanently destroyed for the '72 Games. But Avery Brundage, head of the International Olympic Committee, disagreed.

Brundage ordered a one-day suspension of the competition. On that day a memorial to the slain athletes would be held. Then he ordered the Games to be resumed on the second day. Many people were outraged. But Brundage's order stood.

The Games continued without any further incidents. But there was no joy or excitement for most of the athletes or fans who remained in Munich that year. Most people agreed that the senseless murder of 11 Israeli athletes had left a dark stain on the Olympic movement that could never be removed. ■

Montreal's Olympic Stars

Determined Decathlete

In 1972 Bruce Jenner finished tenth in the Olympic decathlon. It wasn't a great showing. Still, Jenner was pleased. He was young, and this was his first Olympics. He planned on training hard for the next four years. Then he'd try again in 1976.

Four years later at Montreal, Jenner showed that all his hard training had paid off. The first five decathlon events were held on one day. There were two races, the long jump, the shot put, and the high jump. None of them were his best events. Yet, at the end of the day he was in third place in the overall competition.

The following day the final five events were held. Jenner made a great showing in the discus, the pole vault, and the javelin. The 1500-meter race was the final event. By now he had a comfortable lead for the gold medal. Still, he ran the 1500 as if everything were riding on the one race. He finished a strong second.

When the results were announced, the young American had won the decathlon gold medal by more than 200 points. His determination had brought him the title every decathlon champion receives—the "greatest athlete in the world." ■

American track and field star Bruce Jenner won the decathlon at the 1976 Olympics.

Pint-Sized Powerhouse

To many onlookers, 14-year-old gymnast Nadia Comaneci seemed like a doll. She weighed only 88 pounds, and stood barely 5-feet tall.

At the 1976 Olympics, sell-out crowds filled the forum in Montreal to watch her, and that wasn't just because she was so cute. The tiny gymnast from Rumania was a world-class athlete.

She competed on the uneven parallel bars and the balance beam. Her movements were incredibly swift and powerful—but as graceful as a ballet dancer's. She stunned the audience with her perfectly performed flips and somersaults.

No athlete had ever before scored a perfect 10.0 in Olympic gymnastic events. She was the first.

And she didn't achieve just one perfect score—she achieved seven! Young Nadia won more than gold medals in Montreal. She won the hearts of all who saw her perform. ■

Nadia Comaneci shows the true Olympic form that made her a gold medal winner at the 1976 Games.

Hank Aaron—Beating the Babe

Hank Aaron of the Atlanta Braves was thinking fastball. So was Al Downing, the pitcher for the Los Angeles Dodgers.

It was the evening of April 8, 1974. The noise in the Atlanta stadium was deafening. Most people in the ballpark were hoping to see baseball history made that night. In a moment they would get their wish.

Downing started into his motion. The noise from the crowd grew even louder. The pitch came in hard, but Aaron was ready. His swing was perfect.

The ball went sailing out toward left-center field. It rose higher and higher as it traveled. Finally, it reached its peak and started down. It

Hank Aaron hits his 715th career home run to break Babe Ruth's record.

cleared the fence at the 385-foot mark.

On the Atlanta scoreboard a number began to flash. "715!" Aaron smiled as he trotted around the bases. The crowd was screaming with each step he took.

He'd hit many home runs in his two decades of big league baseball. But this one was special. This one was the 715th homer of his career—the one that broke Babe Ruth's all-time home run record. Baseball now had a new home run king—and his name was Hank Aaron. ■

O. J. Simpson— The Juice Hits 2,000 Yards

Entering the 1973 season, many people felt that O. J. Simpson was pro football's best running back. The year before he had led the league in rushing while playing for a

very poor Buffalo Bills team. At age 26, he was just hitting his prime.

But even Simpson's biggest fans weren't prepared for what he accomplished in 1973. Starting with the

season's very first game, he was outstanding. And as the season progressed, he gained more than 200 yards on several occasions.

Then in the final game of the year, Simpson shattered Jim Brown's single-season rushing record of 1,863 yards. For years that record was thought to be unbreakable. But Simpson didn't stop there. By the end of the fourth quarter he had once again gained more than 200 yards in a single game. That gave him a total of 2,003 yards rushing for the season, an incredible accomplishment. The "Juice" stood alone among pro football's running backs. ■

In 1973 O. J. Simpson became the first player in NFL history to rush for more than 2,000 yards in a season.

Billie Jean King winning the 1971 U.S. Open Tennis Championship in Forest Hills, New York.

The 1970 Open Tennis Tournament in Rome was over. The winner of the men's division had a big smile on his face. He had good reason to smile. He'd just been presented with a check for $7,500.

Then the crowd applauded when Billie Jean King's name came over the loudspeaker. She'd just won the women's division. But she wasn't smiling. Her check was only $600!

She wanted to prove a woman was worth as much as a man.

Billie Jean wasn't angry—she was disgusted. It wasn't fair that men got paid so much more than women. Then and there she decided to do something about it. And when Billie Jean made a decision, she stuck to it.

She was born Billie Jean Moffit in 1943 in Long Beach, California. When she was 10, she began playing tennis. In 1959, at age 15, she won a big tournament in California. She went on as far as the national quarterfinals for girls.

In 1960 she went to the nationals again. This time she competed with girls 18 and under. She played well. Finally, though, she lost to 17-year-old Karen Hantze.

In 1961 she was invited to the Wimbledon Championship Tournament in England. It was the world's leading tournament. There, she teamed in doubles with Karen Hantze. The two teenagers won. They were the youngest players ever to win the event.

In 1964, while in college, Billie Jean married Larry King, another student. She continued to play tennis. Every year she improved.

She was voted Female Athlete

Billie Jean King— In Search of Equality

of the Year in 1967. And by the 1970 Tournament in Rome, she'd become the best women's tennis player in the world. She'd won many championships, including 10 Wimbledon titles. Still, she earned less than many low-ranking male tennis players.

The Virginia Slims cigarette company was starting a tennis tour for women. Although Billie Jean disapproved of smoking, she decided to join the tour. She liked the prize money Virginia Slims was offering. But there was something else that

she thought was equally important. She wanted to prove a woman was worth as much as a man. And she soon did.

In 1971 she set a record for women's professional tennis. She won more than $100,000 in a single year. Only a very few male players earned more than that. And Billie Jean was in her prime. There were sure to be many victories ahead for her. And best of all—she'd helped open up possibilities for all women tennis players. ∎

Super Steelers—Four Times Over

In the early 1970s, Art Rooney had earned a reputation he didn't want.

He'd owned the Pittsburgh Steelers football team since 1933. Among owners, he was the "grand old man." But in all his years, his team had never won a championship.

By the end of 1972, though, it looked like things might change. The Steelers hadn't won the championship, but they'd made it to the playoffs.

The Steelers coach, Chuck Noll, was putting together a fine team. Young quarterback Terry Bradshaw was learning fast. Running back Franco Harris showed great promise. Lynn Swann, a pass receiver, had super speed. And Joe Greene was possibly the best defensive tackle in pro football.

In 1973 they made it to the playoffs again. But once again they were bumped.

By 1974 they were ready. Their offense was powerful. Bradshaw and Swann posed a strong threat in the air. And Harris was almost unstopable on the ground.

Perhaps even more impressive was their defensive line. It had Greene, L. C. Greenwood, Ernie Holmes, and Dwight White. They got the nickname "The Steel Curtain."

Champions At Last

The combination of a top offense and defense was too much for their competitors. At the end of the season, Pittsburgh had made it to the Super Bowl.

The Steelers played the Minnesota Vikings in New Orleans on a cold and windy day in January. Most of the game was dominated by defense. When it was over, the Steelers had beaten the Vikings 16–6.

At last they were the NFL champions. Now it was Art Rooney's turn to smile.

The next season the team went to the Super Bowl again. This time, they beat the Dallas Cowboys 21–17. Rooney's smile grew broader.

The Steelers were bumped in the playoffs for the next two years. But then they completed the 1978 season with another Super Bowl victory over Dallas.

They kept up the momentum through 1979. At season's end, they were in the Super Bowl once more. This time, they beat the Los Angeles Rams 31–19.

It was a remarkable feat. They'd won their fourth Super Bowl title in six years.

Rooney could be proud. So could Noll, Bradshaw, Harris, Swann, and the "Steel Curtain." There was no doubt about it. In pro football, the 1970s belonged to the Pittsburgh Steelers. ∎

Lynn Swann's spectacular catches helped the Pittsburgh Steelers beat the Dallas Cowboys in Super Bowl X.

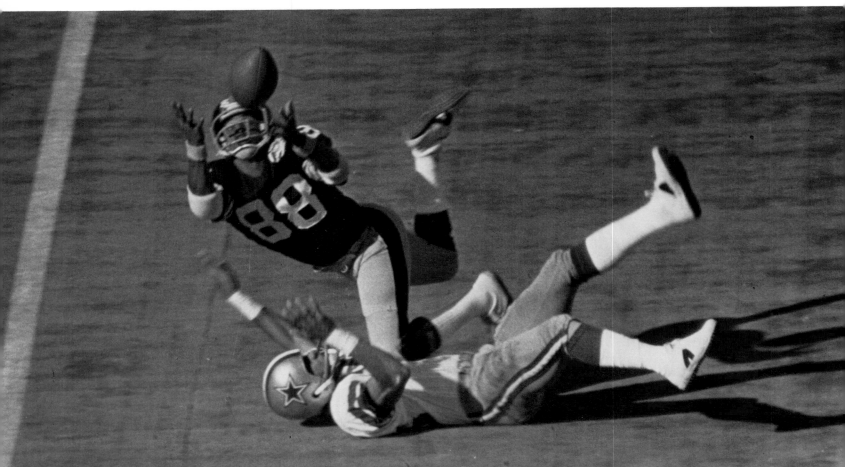

"**I** am the greatest!" Muhammad probably shouted those words several thousand times in his boxing career. The brash, confident fighter had no doubt of his fighting skills. And he made sure that everyone within earshot knew that. In a 15-year pro career filled with great triumphs—and only a few disappointments—very few boxing experts would disagree.

Ali burst upon the boxing scene when he was 18 years old. Fighting under his real name, Cassius Clay, he won the Olympic gold medal for light heavyweights at the 1960 Games in Rome. Shortly after that, he turned professional.

He came to national sports attention in 1964. That year he had fought heavyweight champion Sonny Liston. Before the fight, Clay had boldly predicted victory in his own distinctive way, "Liston will fall in five—that's no jive." Often in his career, Clay's skills in the ring were overshadowed by such predictions and chants. "Float like a butterfly, sting like a bee," was the way he described his own fighting style.

Many people didn't take the cocky young man seriously. Because of his inexperience, Liston was a heavy favorite. But Clay shocked the boxing world by defeating Liston in seven rounds to take the title. A year later he successfully defended his title by defeating Liston again.

Barred from the Ring

For the next three years, Clay defended his title eight times. He won each fight. But in 1967, outside the ring, he lost a big battle. He was convicted of refusing to submit to induction into the armed services. The World Boxing Association then stripped him of his title and barred him from the ring.

Back in 1964 Clay had joined the Black Muslims. Eventually he took a Muslim name, Muhammad Ali. As a Muslim he refused, on religious grounds, to join the armed forces.

Ali appealed his conviction. But

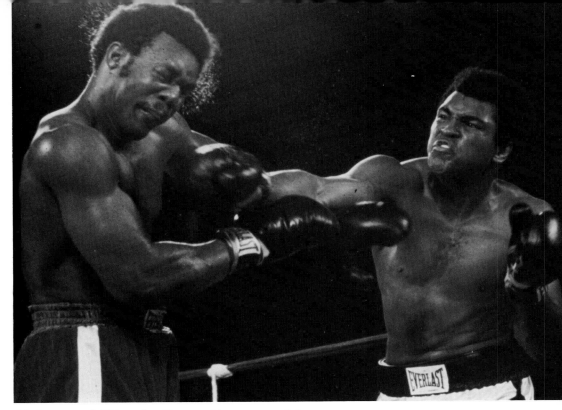

Muhammad Ali rocks George Foreman with a hard right in their 1974 title fight in Zaire.

Muhammad Ali— The Greatest

before the case was resolved, his title was taken away. Joe Frazier became the new heavyweight champ in 1970.

Ali stayed firm in his beliefs. He became a symbol of achievement for people all over the world. Gradually even his harshest critics came to respect his sincerity and to recognize his abilities. But Ali was not through boxing.

In 1971 Ali's conviction was overturned by the U.S. Supreme Court. That same year, he fought Joe Frazier at Madison Square Garden in New York City. Ali was attempting to win back his title. However, the younger and stronger Frazier defeated Ali in a close 15-round decision.

Ali and Frazier were to have two more fights, including the "Thrillah in Manila." Ali won both.

In 1974 the powerful George Foreman was the heavyweight champ. He had taken the title from Frazier the year before. Now Foreman and Ali would meet in a title fight in Zaire, Africa.

Foreman was a strong favorite to retain his title. But the lightning-fast Ali—even at age 32—proved again what a great boxer he was. He knocked out Foreman in the eighth round to regain the heavyweight crown.

Over the next four years, Ali successfully defended his title ten times. By now he was in his late 30s and his skills had only slightly diminished. He continued to amaze boxing experts and fans.

Then in February 1978, Ali lost a stunning decision to a young unknown named Leon Spinks. People said Ali was through, a has-been at 36. But he had one more surprise left. Seven months later he fought Spinks again. This time Ali won a 15-round decision.

With his victory, Ali became the first heavyweight in history to win the title three times.

Ali retired in 1979. When he quit, he was hailed by millions of fight fans as the greatest heavyweight in history and by millions more as an inspirational leader. All around the world, he had become one of the most popular figures of his time. ■

A Musical Genius Remembered

Fame came early to Spanish cellist Pablo Casals. At 23 he made his debut with a major French orchestra. The gifted young man was immediately recognized as a master of his instrument. In the years to come he would also become noted as a conductor, teacher, composer, and pianist.

But music wasn't his whole life. Casals was always dedicated to the cause of peace. He once said, "I am a man first, an artist second."

For 70 years Pablo Casals was considered the greatest cellist in the world.

He was born in Vendrell, Spain, in 1876. As a boy, he learned to play a number of instruments. At 12, he decided the cello would be his main instrument. So he went to Barcelona, Spain, to attend the Municipal School of Music. And there he fell in love with the music of Bach.

In 1894 he studied at the Royal Conservatory in Madrid, Spain. The following year, he moved to Paris. There he became a cellist at the Paris Opera. In 1895 he made his debut with the Lamoureux Orchestra. For the next 70 years, he would be considered the greatest cellist in the world.

During the course of his career, Casals traveled around the world, giving performances. He played with the greatest musicians of his time. His first American appearance was at the White House in Washington, D.C. There, in 1901, he played for President Theodore Roosevelt. Sixty years later he visited the White House again. This time, he played for President John F. Kennedy.

> "I am a man first, an artist second."

When the Spanish Civil War began in 1935, Casals supported the government. He left Spain in 1939, just before Franco came to power. During World War II, Casals lived in Prades, France. France was occupied by the Germans. Casals, though, would have nothing to do with them. He gave concerts to raise money for war victims.

In 1956 he moved to Puerto Rico, his mother's birthplace. There he founded the Casals Festival, a major world musical event. In 1958 he performed for the United Nations in New York City. The concert, like much of his life, was dedicated to peace.

His warmth as a human being showed in his teaching. Once, one of his pupils forgot a piece she knew well. Casals put her at ease. It was all right, he said. "Everything should be new every time you play it." It was for him. He was still playing the cello when he was in his nineties.

When he died in 1973, the world mourned his passing. He was a great artist—and a great man. ∎

Holding flowers, exiled Russian author Alexander Solzhenitsyn is welcomed to the village of Eifel by West German author Heinrich Böll.

A Nobel Writer Is Exiled

The Soviet police came to Alexander Solzhenitsyn's apartment early in the evening. They didn't bother to knock. They just stormed in and arrested him. Solzhenitsyn was taken to prison and charged with treason. The next day, February 13, 1974, he was found guilty. Within hours, he was put on a plane for West Germany.

One of the most popular writers in the world had been banished from his own country. His Soviet citizenship had been taken away. He would be forced to spend the rest of his life in exile. The world was stunned and saddened at Russia's treatment of one of its most noted authors.

Alexander Solzhenitsyn was born in Kislovodsk, Russia, in 1918. During World War II he had fought bravely for the Red Army. After the war, though, he was arrested. In a letter to a friend, Solzhenitsyn had criticized Josef Stalin's government. As a result he was forced to serve eight years in labor camps.

In 1956 he was finally freed. It was then that he began to teach school and to write. In 1962 Solzhenitsyn published his book *One Day in the Life of Ivan Denisovich*. The book was based on his experiences in the labor camps. In it, he criticized Stalin's 25-year leadership of the Soviet Union. At first, the book was accepted by some Soviet leaders. But many people in the government attacked Solzhenitsyn.

International Fame

By 1970 he had published several important books. They included *First Circle* and *Cancer Ward*. Both were critical of the government.

Then in 1970, Solzhenitsyn gained international fame when he won the Nobel Prize for literature. The ceremony was held in Sweden. Solzhenitsyn didn't attend. He feared that if he left his country, he wouldn't be allowed back.

By January 1974, the Communist party was attacking him constantly. In *Pravda*, the party newspaper, they said he had betrayed his own country. The truth was that Solzhenitsyn loved Russia. He had a compelling reason for writing about injustices the Soviet government had caused—he didn't want them to be repeated.

By this time, his work had been published around the world. The leaders of many countries said they would welcome him. They said he would be free to write whatever he wanted.

But his heart was in Russia. He never wanted to leave. However, the decision was no longer his.

Shortly before he was forced to leave Russia, Solzhenitsyn gave words of advice to his countrymen. He urged them to seek the truth. His message to them was simple: "Live not by lies."

After his banishment, Solzhenitsyn settled in Switzerland. In 1976 he moved to the United States. He continued to write and speak out against injustices inside his native country. ∎

A scene from *Fiddler on the Roof*, Broadway's longest-running play.

Fiddler Finally Closes

Farewell to a Broadway Classic

How interesting could a musical about a Russian milkman living in 1900 possibly be? How long could a play like that expect to run on Broadway? Those were the questions theater people were asking in September 1964.

The answer was: longer than any other play in Broadway history.

The fantastically successful musical *Fiddler on the Roof* was written by Joseph Stein. He based it on short stories by Sholom Aleichem. The tales were about Tevye, a Jewish milkman living in Russia around the turn of the century. Like the stories, the musical had great humor. But it also had its grim side. It told of the hardships of Jewish life in a country village. The tsar ruled Russia at the time, and Jews there were often persecuted.

Before *Fiddler* opened, many theater people predicted it wouldn't go far. They said that Jewish audiences in New York might like it. But beyond that, they felt, it would have little appeal.

The show opened on Broadway, September 22, 1964. It was a hit from the start. First it played at the Imperial Theater. There it brought in $88,000 a week. Later, at the larger Majestic Theater, it took in $100,000 a week.

Not only did it make money, critics loved it. The brilliant actor Zero Mostel was the first actor to star as Tevye. Five other actors played that role before the musical's run ended.

The music was composed by Jerry Bock, and Sheldon Harnick wrote the lyrics. The song "If I Were a Rich Man" soon became a classic. *Fiddler* was choreographed by

Jerome Robbins, a Broadway legend. The dance numbers were stunning. They included traditional Jewish dances and lively Russian dances.

Soon productions of *Fiddler* were being staged around the world. The show's appeal went far beyond the Jewish community. *Fiddler* was loved everywhere because its characters were so human. It was a huge success in Israel. And people in Japan and Finland could also identify with *Fiddler's* characters. A citizen of Dublin, Ireland, claimed the musical was universal. He said the show's themes of struggle and courage were just as much Irish as they were Jewish.

On July 2, 1972, *Fiddler* finally closed on Broadway. It had broken all records. The musical with "limited appeal" had run for 3,242 performances. ∎

Music World Loses Two Legends

In 1977, within the space of two months, America lost two of its greatest entertainers. Their careers were as different as their backgrounds and life styles. Yet they shared an impact on American music that very few performers of this century could match.

Elvis Presley—King of Rock 'n' Roll

In 1953 the would-be rock star was one of many. In that year he *paid* $4 to record his first record. But three years later, his recording of "Heartbreak Hotel" struck gold. It sold more than a million copies. And that was just the first of 45 gold records for Elvis Presley.

Elvis's manager, Colonel Tom Parker, claimed responsibility for the singer's success. He once said, "When I found Elvis, the boy had nothing but a million dollars worth of talent. Now he has a million dollars."

Elvis's voice and good looks thrilled many women. He also had a wild way of moving his hips as he sang and played the guitar. Those gyrations earned him the nickname "Elvis the Pelvis."

Besides making records, Elvis appeared in 25 movies. All were big moneymakers. He also starred at nightclubs in Las Vegas.

By the early 1970s, though, the fast life was getting to him. He began keeping to himself. But his popularity was as great as ever. When he did perform, he still drew huge crowds.

Then in August 1977, Elvis suddenly died of a heart ailment. Medical reports later showed that drugs had contributed to his death. The former "King of Rock 'n' Roll" had died at the age of only 42. ∎

Elvis Presley threw his whole body into his performances.

Bing Crosby—The Crooner

In the 1930s, a crooning style was popular with many singers. Before long, though, only one vocalist was known as The Crooner. His name was Bing Crosby. And he became one of the most popular entertainers in the world. For almost 50 years, he starred as a singer, dancer, and actor.

Crosby's movie career was filled with successes. He starred in more than 60 films, most of them musicals and comedies. In 1944 he won an Academy Award for his portrayal of a sensitive priest in *Going My Way*. And, in the movie *Holiday Inn*, he introduced his most famous song, "White Christmas." The Crosby version of the Irving Berlin composition went on to become the most popular Christmas song of all time.

Crosby's movie career also found him teamed with comedian Bob Hope in several films. Together they made a series of "Road" pictures that were big hits.

As a sports lover, Crosby owned part of two major league baseball teams. But his first sports love was golf. The "Crosby Clambake," his annual golf tournament at Pebble Beach, California, was a major event.

Crosby was a wealthy man, and a generous one. For years he freely gave of both his time and his money to many charities. In October 1977, at the age of 72, he suddenly died of a heart attack. For a sportsman, it was a fitting end. He had just finished playing 18 holes of golf. ∎

Bing Crosby, a "crooning" legend, during his heyday in the 1940s.

Richard M. Nixon
Spectacular Rise, Spectacular Fall

President Richard Nixon was the first American president ever to resign from office.

No American politician has ever had a career quite like Richard Nixon's. Certainly many other office holders have risen again after being considered politically "dead." And many have had spectacular successes—only to be followed by spectacular failures.

However, no one but Richard Nixon has ever had as many political "rebirths" in one career. And no one but Nixon has ever risen to as great a height—the presidency—and fallen as dramatically from that height—resignation in disgrace.

Richard Milhous Nixon was born in Yorba Linda, California, in 1913. When he was nine, his family moved to nearby Whittier. Later, Nixon attended college there.

He went on to study law at Duke University in North Carolina. After graduating in 1937, he returned to California to practice law.

Five years later he went to Washington, D.C., to do government work. There he was commissioned as a lieutenant in the navy.

In 1946 some Republicans from California talked him into running for Congress. He waged a nasty campaign, hinting strongly that his opponent was a Communist. It worked. He won the election. He also won a nickname—"Tricky Dick."

In 1950 he was elected as senator in California. Then, in 1952 he ran for vice president on the Republican ticket with Dwight Eisenhower.

During the campaign Nixon was almost dropped from the ticket. Word got out about a "secret fund" he received while a congressman. It had been set up by wealthy Californians.

Nixon decided to head off the scandal. He went on television and gave his "Checkers Speech."

The Nixon's dog, Checkers, had been a gift. Nixon tried to convince people that all his gift taking was innocent. It worked. He remained on the ticket. The Republicans won that year, and again in 1956.

In 1960 Nixon ran for president, but lost a close election to John F. Kennedy. Many people thought his political career was over.

But in 1962 he was back, running for governor of California. He was soundly defeated—and once again his career seemed to be over. In fact, after the election, he said he was retiring from politics. He told the press, "You won't have Nixon to kick around anymore."

Then in 1968 he made another comeback. He won the Republican presidential nomination for the second time. As in 1960, the race was very close. Only this time Nixon won, defeating Hubert Humphrey by 500,000 votes. In 1972 he won re-election by the largest margin in U.S. history—18 million votes.

A Presidency in Ruins

As his second term opened, Nixon seemed to be on top of the world. The war in Southeast Asia was winding down. He had made great progress in bettering relations with China and Russia.

By 1974, though, his presidency was in ruins. Many of his associates were in prison or headed there. It seemed certain that he was part of the Watergate cover-up. After much investigation, the House Judiciary Committee recommended that he be impeached. Rather than face a trial in the Senate, Nixon resigned. He was the first president in America's history to do so. His resignation seemed to bring a final curtain down on one of the most fascinating—and strangest—political careers in U.S. history. ■

A Dynamic Israeli Leader

Golda Meir

Golda Mabovitch could claim three countries as home: Russia, America, and Israel.

She was born in Kiev, Russia, in 1898, but when she was eight, she moved to America. She grew up in Milwaukee, Wisconsin. When it came time for her to attend high school, her parents wouldn't allow it. They thought she should marry and raise a family. So when she was 14, they arranged a marriage for her. She refused to marry. Instead, she left home and went to live with her sister in Denver, Colorado.

In Denver, she started high school and worked afternoons and weekends. And there, she met many Zionists. They were Jews who wanted to make a country of their own. They hoped to build it in what was then Palestine.

After high school, Golda returned to Milwaukee and started teachers college. And in 1917, she married Morris Myerson, whom she'd met in Denver. More and more she became interested in Zionism.

In 1921 she and her husband moved to Palestine. They lived in a kibbutz, a community where everyone shared everything. Land, tools—even clothing—were shared by all.

Golda Myerson was intelligent, hardworking, and she had a gift for organizing people. Soon she became active in leading the kibbutz. Later, she became active with Histadrut, a labor organization.

Next Golda became a leader in the drive to build a Jewish state in Palestine. The British ruled the country then. They tried to keep peace between Arabs and Jews there. It was not an easy job.

In the 1930s, Hitler ruled much of Europe. Since one of his goals was to kill all the Jews, many fled to Palestine. The Arabs complained. They didn't want more Jews there.

So to please the Arabs, the British limited Jewish entry to Palestine.

The Jews in Palestine found that unacceptable. Many countries wouldn't accept Jewish refugees. So the Jewish communities in Palestine offered many people their only hope for survival.

Israel Is Founded

Golda thought the British had no right to set such limits. She said, "Jews were here 2,000 years before the British came." European Jews continued to seek a home in Palestine. Often they had to fight the British as well as the Arabs.

Finally, in 1948, the nation of Israel was established. Golda was one of its founders. There she continued her work, serving in many roles. In 1949 she was appointed minister of labor. In 1956 she became foreign minister and served in that post for ten years. That same year she changed her last name to the Hebrew name Meir.

Three years after leaving the foreign ministry, Golda Meir became prime minister of Israel. She was the first woman to hold that post.

During her time as prime minister, Mrs. Meir traveled widely, meeting with many foreign leaders. She also pressed strongly for a diplomatic peace settlement with Israel's Arab enemies, particularly Egypt.

In that area she was unsuccessful. In 1973 another Arab-Israeli War broke out. This time Israel was unprepared and suffered heavy losses before regrouping its forces.

In the aftermath of the conflict, Prime Minister Meir decided to step down from her post. She had governed for five years and was still extremely popular with all Israelis when she retired.

Golda Meir died in 1978 at the age of 80. She was buried in Jerusalem in the heart of the nation she helped found. ∎

Golda Meir served as Israel's first woman prime minister during the early '70s.

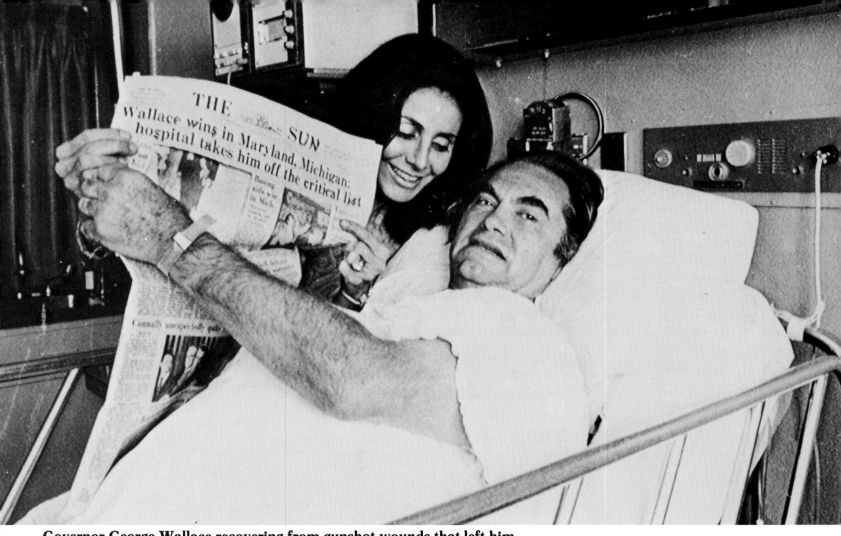

Governor George Wallace recovering from gunshot wounds that left him permanently paralyzed in 1972. His second wife Cornelia is by his side.

A Shattered Dream

George Wallace

In the 1972 presidential primaries, President Richard Nixon had no opposition. The Republican party was going to stay with their "Man in the White House."

For the Democrats it was a different story. As late as mid-May, there was still no clear favorite. Senator George McGovern and former Vice-President Hubert Humphrey were top contenders. Both men were party regulars. But there was a third candidate in the running. He'd run for president before—though not as a Democrat. His name was George Wallace. In 1968 he'd been the candidate of the American Independent party. He wasn't elected that year, but he'd surprised a lot of people by getting nearly 10 million votes. Four years later he decided to seek the Democratic party nomination.

George Corley Wallace was born in Clio, Alabama, in 1919. As a high-school boxer, he held the state's amateur bantamweight title. In law school he earned money by boxing professionally. He graduated from law school in 1942 and joined the Air Force. He served there until the end of World War II.

During the late 1940s, Wallace won his first election to public office. He served two terms in Alabama's state legislature. In 1952 he was elected as a district court judge. In 1958 he ran for governor and lost. But in 1962 he tried again and won.

Succeeded by Wife

As governor, Wallace was a segregationist. He tried to keep blacks from attending the University of Alabama. Because of Alabama law, he couldn't run for two terms in a row. So his wife Lurleen ran in 1966. She

won, but he ran the governor's office. He was elected governor again in 1970.

In his 1968 try for president, Wallace had received 13% of the vote. He had run as an antiliberal candidate of a third party. But in 1972 he thought he might win on the Democratic ticket.

On May 15 that year, Wallace was campaigning in Maryland. After his speech, a man named Arthur Bremer came up to him. "Hey, George," he said, "aren't you going to shake my hand?" As Wallace turned, Bremer raised a pistol and shot him five times.

An ambulance rushed Wallace to the hospital. There, doctors found that a bullet had damaged his spinal cord. He would remain paralyzed from the waist down. His dream of being president was no doubt shattered forever. ∎

Democratic Keynoter

Barbara Jordan

The keynote speech at the 1976 Democratic convention was almost over. It had been a great one. The dynamic speaker finished by quoting Abraham Lincoln:

"As I would not be a slave, I would not be a master. This expresses my idea of democracy. Whatever differs from this, to the extent of the difference, is no democracy."

The audience burst into cheers. They yelled and waved banners. They chanted, "We want Barbara! We want Barbara!" It was a shining moment for the keynote speaker, Barbara Jordan. But it was just one of many in her remarkable career.

Barbara Charline Jordan was born in Houston, Texas, in 1936. Her father was a Baptist minister. She graduated from Texas Southern University in 1956. And in 1959 she earned a law degree from Boston University. Then she returned to Houston and took a job with a law firm. While there, she became active in Democratic party politics.

Twice she tried for a seat in the Texas House of Representatives. She lost in 1962 and again in 1964. In 1966, though, she was elected to the Texas State Senate.

Jordan became the first black congresswoman ever elected from the deep South.

Then, in 1972, Barbara Jordan was elected to the U.S. House of Representatives. She became the first black congresswoman ever elected from the Deep South. She was reelected in 1974 and 1976.

Two years before her 1976 keynote speech, she became a national figure. This came about because of the Watergate hearings. As a member of the House Judiciary Committee, she had impressed people around the country with her intelligence and her manner. Her questions were to the point. She was among those approving articles of impeachment against President Richard Nixon.

After Jimmy Carter was elected president, she met with him. They talked about her serving in his cabinet. But the only position she was interested in was attorney general, and it wasn't offered to her. She was disappointed, but she still had plenty to do. She'd just been reelected to Congress. It turned out that this would be her last term in the House of Representatives. When it was completed, she chose not to seek reelection. Instead, she joined the faculty at the University of Texas in Austin. There, she became a professor in the Lyndon B. Johnson School of Public Affairs. ■

Congresswoman Barbara Jordan and Democratic Chairman Robert Strauss quiet the convention crowd. Jordan is about to deliver the 1976 convention keynote speech.

OUR CENTURY: 1970-1980

GLOSSARY

blackout: a period in which electric power fails, leaving a city or part of a city without power or light.

cease-fire: an agreement made during a war to stop firing, usually so that negotiations can be carried out between the warring sides.

civil war: a war between different groups of people within the same country.

Cold War: a war fought with words and propaganda between the governments of the United States and the Soviet Union after World War II.

cover-up: an attempt to hide, or "cover-up," a mistake or illegal activity.

cult: a group of people who live together, obeying the orders and leadership of one person who often claims to be in touch with god.

desegregation: efforts and practices to remove restrictions that separate blacks and whites.

impeachment: a legal procedure for removing a president or other high official from office.

perjury: the crime of lying under oath in a court of law.

POW camp: a place where prisoners of war, usually soldiers, are kept until the end of the war.

Sandinistas: the organized popular movement that overthrew the dictatorship of Anastasio Somoza in Nicaragua. The group takes its name from a martyred freedom fighter, Sandino.

terrorists: people who commit acts of violence in order to try to achieve their political aims.

test-tube baby: a child conceived by combining its mother's ovum and father's sperm outside the mother's body.

Vietcong: guerilla fighters during the Vietnam War who opposed the South Vietnamese government.

walkout: a situation that occurs when a group of workers agrees to walk off a job at a certain time to register protest.

Watergate 7: seven men who took part in the Watergate burglary and other illegal activities while serving the Nixon White House.

wiretapping: placing a listening device on a telephone so one can record or listen in on other people's conversations.

Yom Kippur: the "Day of Atonement," the holiest Jewish holiday.

BOOKS FOR FURTHER READING

The titles listed below provide more detailed information about some of the people and events described in this book. Ask for them at your local library or bookstore.

The Nineteen-Seventies. Healey (Franklin Watts)

One Giant Leap for Mankind. Smith (Silver Burdett)

Richard M. Nixon: The Thirty-seventh President. Hargrove (Childrens Press)

The United States in the Vietnam War. Lawson (Harper Children's Books)

What was Watergate? Kilian (St. Martin's Press)

PLACES TO WRITE OR VISIT

Communications Hall of Fame
72 Mountain Street
Sutton, Quebec J0E 2K0

National Afro-American Museum
& Cultural Center
1350 Brush Row Road
P.O. Box 578
Wilberforce, OH 453384

National Air & Space Museum
Sixth Street & Independence
Avenue
Washington, D.C. 20560

INDEX